LEAN THINK

LEAN THINK

Revolutionizing Education by Doing Less

Julie Laub

Lean Think: Revolutionizing Education by Doing Less

Copyright ©2021 Julie Laub

Edited by Linda Lawliss

Visit the author at LeanThink.org

ISBN-13: 978-0-578-95511-7

Printed in the United States of America

First Edition

Dedication

The book is dedicated to my wonderful husband, Samuel Gregg
Laub. He understands Lean Think better than anyone on the
planet.

Table of Contents

Preface

Welcome to Lean Think! In these pages, you will join me in my Lean journey so you can begin your own. The key word throughout this experience is *incremental*. Step by step, you will uncover nuggets of gold you can immediately use in your teaching.

The goal for any teacher is to be the best teacher possible, enabling students to knock it out of the ballpark, learn, and be inspired. Lean, a process improvement ideology created in manufacturing, provides an effective approach to accomplish that goal and adds the possibility to do it all in contract time. People chuckle when they hear the last sentence – that goal seems impossible. But trust me, the tools provided by Lean Think help make a teacher better, and students perform at a higher level in less time. While the goal is lofty, classroom practices indeed get better … incrementally.

I have three recommendations to get the most out of this book. First, there is a lot of information so read the book through once, then use it as a reference. As you initially read chapters on organization, waste, and tools, jot down notes. Highlight at least one action item you can integrate into your classroom practices from each section. Take your time; this is not a race. Then prioritize, implement, and observe the impact it has on you and your students. Do this step by step, one action at a time. (Hint: Remove waste before applying tools for the quickest win. It also opens space to utilize Lean Think tools.) Teachers attending Lean Think workshops find this careful integration is the best way to affect immediate change.

Second, be aware that Lean Think applies to every facet of life, because everything in life is a process. You will catch yourself saying, "I can use this at home." I encourage you to take these principles and find ways to incorporate them into everyday life. They foster an improvement mindset and language that flows naturally, regardless of setting — home or work.

Lastly, enjoy the journey! Make it more like a game to see how well your students can do, with the added victory of going home on time. It is a captivating experiment that will yield huge gains, including leaps in success, gratitude, and overall classroom contentment. Ultimately, you will discover how to do less and get more with Lean Think!

Introduction: Sink or Swim

I never imagined myself a teacher. I loved science and math, visualizing a STEM field as a career. My dad planted a specific love for chemistry in the heart of a 12-year-old child. For a school science project, he took me to his place of work, the local power plant. He worked as a lab technician and got me a pass, providing a tour of the plant and proudly introducing me to his coworkers and managers. We ate lunch and, best of all, did chemistry "experiments" together. He taught me how to run the laboratory tests, and our last experiment was a titration, a common but powerful laboratory technique to determine the pH of solutions, water in this case. Drop by drop, I added sodium hydroxide from the delicate burette. Flashes of pink swirled as the solution changed, exciting my curiosity. With one drop, the entire solution turned vibrant hot pink and stayed pink. From that moment, I loved chemistry.

In my first year of college at the College of Eastern Utah, my chemistry professor, Stephen Ott, sealed the deal. He was an outstanding, articulate, and kind instructor, making chemistry interesting and easy to understand. As a result, I declared a chemistry major, transferred to the University of Utah upon earning an Associates of Arts from CEU, and struggled through a tough core science degree. Two and a half years later, diploma in hand, I began working at DataChem Laboratories in Salt Lake City, UT. I worked as an Organic Chemist II in the Gas Chromatograph/Mass Spectrometry Semi-Volatile department.

Try saying that fast, three times in a row! I loved it and gained invaluable knowledge with priceless experience.

Three years later, I gave birth to my first baby girl. Growing up, well-meaning teachers and mentors told me, "You can have it all, career and family." But leaving my sweet baby girl every day while I went to work convinced me I did not want it all. So, I set my career aside and got busy raising a family. Fifteen years and five darling daughters later, I had served as a Room Mother more times than I could count, volunteered at the elementary school 1-3 times a week, baked cookies, made playdough, shuttled kids to every conceivable practice, and happily ran a bustling household.

On August 31, 2010, while celebrating my youngest daughter's 8th birthday, life pivoted. My dad approached me and said he and my mom always thought I would be a good teacher. Had I thought about going back to school? If so, they would pay for my continuing education. Who could pass up that offer? Because of my parents' financial gift and my family's emotional support, in December 2011, I graduated with a Master's of Art in Teaching Science from Western Governors University.

Even before I graduated with my MA and teaching credentials, a miraculous door opened at Clearfield High School in Davis School District in fall 2011. Amazingly, I was hired as the advanced chemistry instructor teaching Advanced Placement, International Baccalaureate Standard Level, Pre-IB, and Honors Chemistry. My first-year teaching not only required curriculum design and content creation, lesson planning and classroom management, but also a master's degree project and course work. All the while, my incredible husband, Gregg, and five sweet girls, ages ranging from 9 to 15, discovered new ways to make our lives work.

Even now, I feel ill remembering the insane amount of work! Drowning, gasping for air, and surviving is the best description of my first-year teaching. But many teachers can attest to a similar early teaching experience. I created every assignment, lab, test, demonstration, and activity for four different preps (content courses) from scratch. Even after I completed my master's degree, I spent huge amounts of time outside of school. I worked late into the night, got up early, and hauled books back and forth from school to home. Even though I turned off my job for five hours a day, from the time I picked up junior high carpool at 3:00 p.m. until my adorable girls slept at 8:00 p.m., the remaining 19 hours faded into an abyss of teacher work.

My husband and I knew it would be hard; we just did not know how hard. To make things even harder, the school year began with a sniper shooting at the football team one afternoon at practice. Second term, a student set off a bomb in the cafeteria vending machines. Then, third term changed my life: One of my beautiful students, the junior class president who occupied the first-row, front desk during second period honors chemistry, took his life. I still fight tears every time I think of my student Sam.

Exhausted in every way possible, my first 40 teaching weeks came to an end. Despite the challenges and sleep deprivation, I loved teaching. I had found a niche. Talking to an assistant principal, I told him I knew why teachers taught … because of the students. Coupled with my passion for chemistry and newfound joy of growing and supporting young minds, a sense of purpose and vision filled me. The framed teaching motto hanging in my chemistry classroom 2314 summarizes these emotions: I love who I teach and what I teach.

Enter Lean

That first summer after I taught Clearfield students, my daughters' high school offered me a job. Even though I was sad to leave my first school, I was grateful for the new opportunity and transferred to Davis High School. Embracing the fresh start, I hoped the second year of teaching would prove infinitely easier. However, much to my surprise and the chagrin of my husband, my work hours did not change. Outside of my children's waking hours at home, schoolwork consumed me. In October 2012, my husband intervened. He told me such a lifestyle offered no sustainability and insisted I quit if teaching looked like this for our family. Then, very emphatically, he said, "You need Lean."

I had heard Gregg, my husband, throw the term "Lean" around for years. He is an electrical engineer working for a safety organization as a Lead Field Engineer, inspecting manufacturers' products and processes for compliance with safety standards. Most, if not all, of his hundreds of clients use Lean in the workplace, but that was the extent of my knowledge on the term.

A critical moment transpired when Gregg told me I needed Lean. I felt desperate, so I wholeheartedly agreed with him. Anything was better than what my family, students, and I were limping our way through. So, with an open heart and mind I said, "Teach me." Over the next several months, Gregg coached me in the Lean ideology and approach. I constantly asked the question, "Does this add value?" To everything my students and I touched and did, I applied that question as a filter. Often, I asked Gregg, "Do you think this adds value?" He would patiently walk me through the steps of remembering the customer, goal, and measure. He consistently moved through the Lean ideology and repeatedly helped me remove waste or implement Lean tools.

The first victory happened five months later in March 2013. By 8:00 p.m., I had completed everything on my list for both work and home tasks. Thrilled, I found Gregg in his office and asked, "Do you want to go for a walk or watch something?" I can picture his face perfectly. He looked straight at me with his crystal-clear blue eyes and said, "I have my wife back."

This significant win for our family cultivated peace and a sense of normalcy in the household. Thanks to my husband, I discovered a mechanism to help control my time. I used manufacturing principles to radically change the way I approached every facet of education. It enabled me to effectively manage time and resources to balance all aspects of my life as a wife, mother, and teacher.

Two More Surprises

Unexpectedly, Lean brought two more benefits. Recall, my first-year teaching was difficult for many reasons. The students knew I cared for and loved them dearly, but I wanted more. Always, I want to be the best, and I want my students to be the best. I worked hard to teach all students chemistry and help them master it. Unfortunately, not as much learning happened in my classroom that first year as I had hoped. While my honors and pre-IB students solidly hit an 83% proficiency rate on the state standardized chemistry test (CRT at the time), and all my IB students passed the Chemistry Standard Level exam with a 4 or better, AP proved a different animal. The AP chemistry pass rate posted an abysmal 25%, which meant only 1 in 4 students passed the test. When I opened the results in July 2012, I cried and emailed my principal. I promised to do better the next year for those brave students enrolling in AP chemistry.

The second year rolled around, and a few other variables changed in my career. As previously mentioned, I transferred to Davis High School where my daughters attended. (I taught all but one daughter, and three daughters took three different chemistry classes from me – what joy!) Davis High boasts an affluent student population and tremendous parental support. Additionally, the previous year's preps downsized from four to two; initially, I only taught honors and AP chemistry at Davis High. Certainly, both the student population and decreased workload positively aided my second-year teaching experience. Even with new variables, the end-of-year numbers revealed gains beyond the impact of changing schools. Of course, I attribute that to implementing Lean into my teaching.

Utilizing Lean principles for six months of the second teaching year gave me control of my time and stopped the downward spiral, which goes down as my first victory with Lean. The second win was a surprise. My students performed better, a lot better. The honors students earned a 90% overall pass rate, a 7% increase over the previous year — probably due mostly to the different demographic. But the AP chemistry score improvement was shocking by comparison. Recall the first-year pass rate barely hit 25%. The second-year pass rate was a stunning 79%. Could a slightly different demographic in the same district make a 54% difference? I inquired about past years' performances for the school only to discover a 50%-60% pass rate. Clearly, something remarkable changed in my classroom because of Lean. High-level learning occurred. Not only had I literally worked fewer hours, but my students also learned more. Sold by the data, both in my life experience and student performance, I zealously embraced Lean as an innovative mindset posed to revolutionize education.

Yet another surprise is how Lean positively impacted my team and ignited a fire. In spring of 2015, the Utah State Board of Education mandated every student take the SAGE Standardized test, and my Chemistry Professional Learning Community (PLC) saw dismal results. Although the teachers in the PLC all worked hard to help students succeed, as a team, we missed the mark. We had good intentions, but we seemed to be working in opposite directions without any sort of unity to guide our students and to create an effective learning community amongst ourselves.

Our SAGE scores confirmed our struggles. SAGE scores range from 1-4, with 3 and 4 meaning proficient and highly proficient respectively. A 3 or better on the exam is considered a pass, indicating students mastered basic high school chemistry content. On our first SAGE test, the Davis High chemistry population only earned 63%. One out of every 3 students did not pass a basic chemistry exam. A closer look revealed even worse results: The honors chemistry students rocked a 94% pass but our large general chemistry population hobbled in with a 37% pass. Two out of every 3 general chemistry students could not pass the standardized test. We were devastated by these results.

It just so happened the Davis High Community Council sponsored a Lean Education workshop that same summer. I asked my colleagues if we could attend the event together in hopes of gleaning tools to help our team. I work with wonderful people, so I was not taken aback when they gladly accepted the invitation. At the conclusion of the two-day workshop, I asked what they thought about implementing Lean as a team, and without hesitation, everyone jumped on board.

With a firm commitment and open hearts, we applied Lean principles for nine months in our chemistry PLC. In spring of 2016, we held our breath as students took the chemistry SAGE test: our second test iteration and first Lean experiment as a team. Second year SAGE data showed unmistakable success. Overall, the chemistry PLC moved from a 63% to 69% pass — a slight but concrete improvement. The real victories, however, occurred in general chemistry class results with the general chemistry population increasing from a 37% to 56% pass, a whopping 19% increase. That translated into 60 more students achieving mastery of basic chemistry than in the previous year. Additionally, individual teachers saw tremendous gains. One teacher improved from a 29% to 46% pass rate, and another teacher from a 45% to an astounding 77% pass in general chemistry students.

The irony is we did not add anything to our classroom instruction. We did not create new resources, the common response in education when solving a problem. The focus of our team, instead, was waste removal. We spent most of our efforts removing waste and focused only on what we were already doing that added value, key principles in Lean.

Systematic Impact

Accidently, I fell into the first opportunity to share Lean. It arose from a desperate need within my own Chemistry Professional Learning Community at Davis High. Turns out, the chemistry PLC experiment provided the kindling for Lean to spread. I officially began hosting what I dubbed Lean Think workshops, the clever marriage between an industry's process improvement methodology and education. Opportunities to host Lean Think workshops came from the State Board of Education, my home district, numerous elementary schools, and many teacher groups.

Since holding these workshops, I have discovered Lean Think is transferrable and results are reproducible. Elementary and secondary classrooms, content and grade level teams, entire schools, district and state departments, and most importantly, individual teachers implementing Lean Think all experience the positive impacts of focused value. The highlight of all data collected from these groups in the last five years comes from a cluster of four elementary schools. Together they attended a Lean Think workshop summer of 2018. With concerted effort, common language, and a unifying goal, each school systematically integrated Lean Think practices the school year of 2018-2019. At the conclusion of the year, teachers from these four elementary schools observed an 86% increase in student engagement and 74% of teachers reported measurable increase in student academic performance. Any school would happily tout such an increase in engagement and performance. Here is the gem, however, and what makes Lean Think so powerful and unique: An impressive 60% of teachers went home 30-120 minutes earlier EVERY DAY. An unbelievable 91% of teachers reported an increase in job satisfaction! And why not? They spent less time working for free and their students learned more!

Therein lies the strength of Lean in education. Teachers do less and students learn more. Teachers spend countless unpaid hours before and after school and during summer months striving for student achievement. Tell teachers they can have back part of their personal lives and, no worries, their students will learn even more in their classrooms? Good luck. Their response would be the same as if you told them that you developed cold fusion or alchemy. However, with Lean Think, that miracle of giving teachers back their personal time and students excelling can happen.

I never imagined myself a teacher, but I am so glad I bear that proud title. I love teaching students, and now I love teaching teachers. Sharing the beauty and potency of Lean Think has changed the lives of educators and, by association, their students. Lean Think practitioners use the principles every day, continually perfecting them as part of a captivating game to see how efficiently and effectively we can craft education to enable students to reach new levels of success.

Chapter 1: So, What Is Lean?

Lean for Dummies defines Lean as, "[a] holistic and sustainable approach to using less of everything to give you more" (Sayer, 2012). Similar, but carrying an educational angle, *Optimizing Student Learning* defines Lean as, "[m]aking obvious what adds value by reducing everything else. Doing more with less" (Ziskovsky, 2010). I discovered Lean is a culture of incremental process improvement where people are valued. The advantage of Lean lies in the fact that everything is a process. The way you tie your shoes, drive to work, cook food, teach a lesson, correct an assignment … everything is a process. Therefore, Lean applies to everything in life. We simply do two things: Look at a process to first, remove waste, and second, sharpen that process. Begin by tackling one step in the process, remove waste, and then sharpen. When that improves, move to another step and do the same, and so on and so forth. Fixed within process improvement are people's voices: hearing and applying the desires of customers and ideas of workers.

To fully grasp the heart of Lean, a look at its backstory is enlightening. Lean's roots come from Benjamin Franklin and his famous adage, "A penny saved is a penny earned." The actual quote originated in the 1737 *Poor Richard's Almanac* where Franklin foreshadowed Lean principles stating, "A penny saved is two pence clear. A pin a-day is a groat a-year. Save and have." In other words, if you do not have to invest money or resources to produce the same outcome, it is as if you earned, or paid yourself, the money and resources you would have spent otherwise.

Building on this principle, forerunners to Lean practices appeared in late 19th century Taylorism and on Henry Ford's production line, revolutionary ideas that suggested manufacturing processes can employ scientific management. The push to increase factory efficiency led to a system evaluating individual steps in a process to identify specialized, repetitive tasks. Consideration for the worker entered the stage. Obviously, questions like "What is the best way to do this?" or "What are the most effective tools?" reverberated in factories. Fred W. Taylor, however, was the first to ask how to incentivize the worker for optimal performance. Rather than treat labor as merely another cost, the worker garnered respect as a fellow human.

Lean gained traction when a brilliant American engineer, Dr. W. Edwards Deming, lectured in Tokyo at the Hakone Convention Center in August 1950. While in Japan, still rising from the ashes of World War II, General Douglas MacArthur asked Deming to help oversee the upcoming 1951 Japanese census. Deming's expertise in quality control techniques brought an invitation from the Union of Japanese Scientists and Engineers to train national scholars. Teaching statistical control, Deming's chief message centered on improving quality to reduce expenses, which would increase productivity and market share. These seeds took hold in the fertile soil rebuilding Japan. Deming is credited as a key champion of the "Japanese Post-War Miracle" as Japan rose from devastation to become one of the world's largest economies.

As the quality culture swept through Japanese manufacturing, a small, near-bankrupt motor company began studying the writings of Deming. The visionary engineer embracing quality, Taiichi Ohno, then pioneered what came to be known as the Toyota Production System (TPS). Ohno, now called the Father of Lean, is quoted as saying, "My biggest contribution was to build a production system that could respond without waste to market changes and, additionally, by its very nature reduce costs" (Supermelon, 2021). In 2008, Toyota Motor Corporation surpassed General Motors as the number one car manufacturer in the world.

The incredible success of the TPS caught the attention of academia in the 1980s. John Krafcik, a Massachusetts Institute of Technology (MIT) graduate student working on research for a James Womack book, coined the term "Lean" in 1988. It is not an acronym, but rather one syllable that embodies the meaning of the TPS. In 1991, James Womack and Daniel Jones published their MIT automotive industry research in the book *The Machine that Changed the World*.

Fueled by the book, Lean Manufacturing rapidly spread through American manufacturing. By 2010, 70% of American manufacturers utilized Lean Manufacturing practices (Woods, n.d.). Since the explosion of Lean in manufacturing, implementation into other industries has proliferated: medicine, military, government, technology (known as Agile), financial services, construction, and late to the party but arriving, education.

Lean Think Baby Steps

The intersection of Lean Manufacturing and education produces Lean Think and accomplishes two fundamental tasks in an educational setting. First, students perform better, learn more, and enjoy a fulfilling school experience. Second, the teacher achieves the above goals in a timely manner within contract time. Simply put, students get more, and teachers do less because the focus is what adds value to the student.

Lean in education is best implemented by what I term, "Lean Think Baby Steps." Lean Think Baby Steps offer a straightforward and uncomplicated methodology to implement Lean Think into any classroom or educational institution. Future chapters look at each step of Lean Think implementation.

LEAN THINK BABY STEPS

- Define: Customer, Goal, and Measure
- Identify: Current and Future states
- Get Organized: 6S
- Kaizen: Incremental Process Improvement
  - Remove Waste
  - Apply Lean Tools
- Plan, Do, Check, Adjust

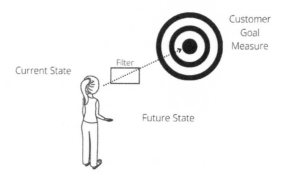

A teacher first defines who their customer is (the students), what the goal for the class is, and how the goal will be measured. The teacher then identifies where they are, the current state, and where they are going, the future state. I imagine the customer, goal, and measure placed in front of the teacher, just out of reach, like a target. The current and future states are on the sides of the teacher. The left hand, stretched out to the side of the teacher, represents the current state of where the teacher is beginning right now. The teacher stretches out their right hand to the other side of their body to symbolize where they want to go, the future state. The distance between their hands shows the ground needed to cover. Incrementally, the teacher will close the gap between the current and future states by process improvement (symbolized by the left hand moving closer to the right hand). Overall, parameters are set

4

with the customer, goal, and measure as the target, and a path is established between the current and future states.

Parameters in place, the teacher begins organization, a mechanism called 6S. 6S stands for six words that begin with the letter S. Catchy, I know, like something a teacher would think of!

- Sort
- Straighten
- Scrub
- Systemize
- Standardize
- Safety

A favorite of teachers, 6S liberates teachers to get rid of stuff, and, boy, do teachers have piles of stuff! The benefit of setting the parameters and getting organized is they are a "one and done." And once the 6S process is complete, the parameters and organization maintain themselves with only occasional outside tweaks.

At this point, the real work begins, moving from the current state to the ideal state one step at a time. (I use the terms Future State and Ideal State interchangeably in the book.) Lean uses a Japanese word to describe this process, *kaizen*, which means incremental process improvement that happens in two ways. First, remove waste, anything that does not add value. With Lean Think eyes, the volume of unearthed classroom waste astounds even the most masterful teacher: used books, outdated files, obsolete equipment; the list goes on and on. Second, incorporate Lean Think tools. Lean Think tools optimize efficiency and effectiveness of classroom resources by assisting in curriculum mapping, standardization, pacing, content creation, and increased educational quality.

Pulling it all together through continual improvement is the Plan, Do, Check, Adjust model, which resembles the scientific process.

Identify a step in a process that needs improvement (*Plan*). Experiment (*Do*) by removing waste or implementing a new tool, like load leveling, for example (see Chapter 13). Collect data and compare it to the goal and measure (*Check*). Based on the results, keep it, trash it, or tweak it (*Adjust*). Then the process begins all over again: Plan, Do, Check, Adjust.

To delve into the specifics of these basic principles and steps, the rest of the book is divided into four sections:

Part I Fundamentals — Setting up the parameters and organization: Chapters 2-6

Part II Waste — Identifying waste and how to remove it: Chapter 7-12

Part III Lean Think Tools — Learning about Lean Think tools and how to use them: Chapters 13-19

Part IV Summary — Pulling it all together: Chapter 20

PART I: Fundamentals

Chapter 2: Who, What, and How

In Lean Think, we begin with Define: Customer, Goal, and Measure. The teacher defines the customer, goal, and measure, which becomes a target that receives laser focus, centered squarely in front of her. This established target lays the foundation for all the teacher will do, and it provides a clear place to circle back to when questions arise.

Who Is the Customer?

Imagine a car manufacturer board meeting. Around whom or what does the meeting center? Figures on how to increase profits? Ideas for innovation? Changes for streamlining? Perhaps, but who is at the center of every issue? The customer, the person who buys the car. Profits only increase if customers buy their cars. No one cares about innovations if the customer is not willing to pay for them. Streamlining only benefits the company if it improves car quality that entices the customer to purchase it. Ultimately, every decision is made for the customer.

Who is the customer in education? The STUDENT. This is obvious and easy to answer. However, the idea of the student as customer is not easily protected. Everyone thinks they are the customer in education. Think of those who might lay claim to the title of customer in your classroom. One demanding group is parents. Then consider administration, fellow teachers, district leadership, state board of education, taxpayers, and society at large.

All claim to have a share in classroom education for various reasons. Society and taxpayers remind the leadership in education that they pay the bills. The state board and district leadership tell teachers what the rules are. Parents are ultimately responsible for their minor children, so they have a right to monitor content and policies. Administrators and peers call for unity and standardization. All of these scenarios are accurate, but none of these groups are the customer.

To determine the true customer, consider the product. What do teachers sell or produce like a car manufacturer produces and sells cars? STUDENT LEARNING. The student is undeniably the customer because they directly receive the educational product of student learning. Whether you are the state superintendent or a high school chemistry teacher, the student is always the customer, and the product is always student learning.

The well-meaning groups, overtly or subconsciously, vying for the customer position in your classroom have a vested interest. Their concern for the student (customer) and student learning (product) account for their interaction and voice in the classroom. However, they must be placed in their proper position as STAKEHOLDERS. Industry stakeholders genuinely care about what happens in a company because it impacts the bottom line. Education stakeholders care about what happens in the classroom because they are entrusted with the health, well-being, and growth of children. However, the stakeholder does not directly receive the product, in industry or education. The only person to receive the education product of student learning is the student. Therefore, every decision made at every level of education must be made for the student!

This perspective changes classrooms, school board meetings, and legislation. What adds value to the STUDENT? What protects the STUDENT? What improves STUDENT learning? As a teacher, every decision I make is for the student. I do not make decisions for parents, coworkers, administration, district/state leadership, or society. I make decisions to increase learning for my students within the laws and guidelines provided by society, educational leadership, and parent expectations. It is in my everyday teaching of designing assignments, labs, activities, and exams that I constantly ask, "Does this add value to my … STUDENT … for them to learn and master the content?" I teach the state curriculum, follow tenured professors' outlines, and adhere to the Advanced Placement Framework to provide the very best for them.

Many positions in education juggle multiple customers. Only teachers exclusively work for a single and primary customer, the student. Administrators create products intended for several different audiences, namely, teachers, parents, and district leadership. Because these groups receive information, data, and direction from administration, they qualify as customers of the administration, but the student is always the PRIMARY customer. High school counselors are another excellent example of a group that works with multiple customers. High School counselors provide information and resources for junior high schools, colleges, parents, and faculty. Yet, their PRIMARY customer is always the student. Decisions for all secondary customers are made with the primary customer in mind, the student.

Just like in industry, the customer drives decisions. Teachers must circle back and remind themselves that they are working for the student. Especially when debate ensues, questions arise, or special allocation requests hit teachers' desks, the focus must always be on the student. Every decision should add value to the student and their learning experience. Sometimes that means a pivot in original plans, and other times it means to simply persevere. Determining when to stand or when to bend depends on what adds the most value to the student.

What Is the Goal?

A goal is essential for forward movement. My darling twins adored turtles and tortoises as children. As a result, they housed three green-shelled reptiles in their shared room throughout elementary school. Though slow moving, when the girls brought the turtle and tortoises outside, Cesar, CeCe, and Candance beelined it for foliage, trying to escape the clutches of human captivity. Their scale clad, one-inch legs propelled their shells forward at a surprising clip, clearly communicating their goal to secure freedom.

What is the goal for your customer? Is it obvious like a turtle running toward petunias to hide in? Is it clearly stated? Notice, the goal is not designed for you; it is for your customer. Every classroom, PLC, department, school, district, and state needs an overarching goal for their customers. The goal in my high school chemistry class is twofold: 1) All students will learn chemistry to mastery; 2) All students will have a positive experience in my chemistry class. I do not want to kill science and curiosity in one fell swoop — I have seen it done. Consider the implied future state reference. In the future state, ALL students reach mastery, and ALL students have a positive experience. Will such a lofty goal ever be achieved 100%? Probably not, but with the goal in place, students get closer and closer every year through incremental process improvement.

To shape the goal another way, ask yourself what you want students to take with them after sitting in your class? What do you want them to remember or be able to do in the next year's math, English, history, art, or science class? What skills or knowledge do they need to be successful in life, college, or in their next grade? What do you want them to remember or do 10 years from now because they were in your class, school, or district? Distill the substance of your classroom content and skills into one or two statements. You have your goal.

Consider an interesting sidenote on creating a classroom goal. In industry, the customer determines the goal. Someone in the market for a dishwasher dictates the goal of the manufacturer, so the company focuses on exactly what the customer wants for the price they are willing to pay. Because students are minors, teachers design the goal. Believe me, no student walks into my classroom saying, "I find chemistry valuable in all aspects of life, and I want to master chemistry while having a wonderful, positive experience." Please send me that child if they exist. Yet, students leave my class loving chemistry and had a great experience, even though they did not come into my classroom with such an attitude. Teachers fashion the goal based on their expertise and experience with both students and content. Students do not know what they do not know. Need some examples of classroom goals?

Rapid Fire: Classroom Goals

- First grade class: Students will be able to read the 500 most common words by sight, read/comprehend 2.1 book level, and write complete sentences. Students will be able to add and subtract two-digit numbers and count money.
- Third grade class: Student will obtain all skills and knowledge needed to be successful in fourth grade.
- Eighth grade English: Students will be able to interpret and summarize inferences.
- Tenth grade history: Students will be able to evaluate primary and secondary documents to write argumentative essays after given a prompt.
- Note: I recommend elementary classrooms write individual goals for each content area. Please also consider writing an experiential or life skill goal as part of the overarching classroom goal.

The above classroom goals apply to the entire course and year. Next, macro-goals provide one or two significant improvements to be executed throughout the year. These are derived from student feedback and data from the previous year. Like a mind map, macro-goals branch off the overarching classroom goal. For example, this year my AP chemistry goal switched pencil and paper textbook homework to a new online e-book platform. My macro-goal for CE chemistry required that I type all lectures notes to post daily with enrichment videos for students who need additional help or who are absent. Every year I write and fulfill 1-2 macro-goals for each prep I teach. Every year my classroom gets closer to ALL students achieving mastery and having a positive experience. Here are some macro-goal ideas.

Rapid Fire: Macro-Goals

- Remove waste from every teaching aspect
- Rewrite tests
- Rewrite labs/activities
- Organize all files
- Make a workbook
- Make a rubric for each activity
- Make a detailed key for every exam
- Create rotation stations
- Create calendar on website or Learning Management System
- Polish online classroom resources
- Email parents monthly and save email template
- Email every student's parents at least once in the year with a praise report

Please do not feel overwhelmed by these macro-goals. After I implemented Lean Think and removed waste, I had room in my schedule and classroom for these improvements.

Smaller daily goals can support the larger classroom goal while you're immersed in the minutia of everyday work. Say I want to boost the strength of students' thesis statements. How and when will I accomplish this? Or, let's say I want students to line up quietly within 10 seconds of the bell ringing. How and when will I teach and practice this? These goals still feed into the overarching classroom goal.

Purposefully and intentionally, draft your overarching classroom goal. Sit on it for a couple of days and let it simmer. Then publish the goal. Put in on the wall, type it in the disclosure, email it to the parents. Make the goal as obvious and apparent as a Russian Tortoise "running" for freedom. Repeatedly state the goal as justification for actions and decisions.

How Will Results Be Measured?

The measure is vitally important. No one needs to convince a teacher of the importance of collecting data. Almost like second nature, assessment flows out of teachers. Get out your red pen and begin grading! Teachers love to write that high score and red smiley face at the top of the page. But dread fills a teacher's heart when red corrective comments overwhelm the margins. Yet, the red marks determine if the goal was reached on an assignment. Likewise, with regard to the overarching classroom goal, the measure to determine whether or not the class has met that goal needs to directly correlate to it. In other words, the measure also needs to be overarching.

I typically use end-of-year assessments as the measure for my goal. Recall, my first goal for high school chemistry is for students to learn chemistry. When I began teaching, I used what was called the State of Utah CRT End of Year Chemistry Exam as my measure. The CRT Exam was then replaced with the SAGE test (which I much preferred due to its adaptive and experiential components). Unfortunately, the SAGE exam was phased out and replaced with the ACT test. The ACT test is a solid measure of data interpretation skills but by no means an assessment of chemistry understanding or application.

My school chemistry PLC and I, therefore, created our own measure. We wrote an 80 multiple-choice question exam covering every core topic in our curriculum. As we know, multiple choice questions can lack depth, problem-solving techniques, and tactile skill evaluation. So, we designed an additional lab practicum exam. With terror in their eyes, students draw 1 of 8 lab prompts from a beaker as I stand at the door. (I'm not ashamed to admit there is something enjoyable about this moment.) With 90 minutes, students design a lab to address the prompt, perform the experiment, collect data, present the results, draw conclusions, and offer an evaluation. Yes, it sounds daunting, but the students execute the lab practicum beautifully. Performing nearly 20 labs within nine months, they knock the final experiment out of the ballpark. Again, joy fills my heart to watch them succeed despite their trepidation. Our measure for the classroom goal is now a two-day event. Day one, students take the multiple-choice test, and day two, they perform the lab practicum, demonstrating they have mastered the material and (hopefully) enjoyed a positive experience with chemistry. Obviously, the measure reflects each student's personal learning experience and individually answers the question, "Did I master high school chemistry?" Collectively, however, the two-day exam informs me as a teacher and our team as a PLC if we achieved the goal of ALL students mastering high school chemistry.

The purpose of the measure reveals how close we came to achieving the goal, or if the goal was achieved at all. Assessing performance against fixed criteria reveals strengths and weaknesses. Without the measure, the feedback loop breaks, and changes are unidentifiable as positive or negative. The goal only works to increase student performance when a quantifiable measure illuminates whether or not practices attain the goal.

Of course, peppered throughout the year are numerous formative and summative assessments/labs, administered in preparation for the end-of-year exam. The final exam provides one cumulative data set by which to measure student performance overall. This then drives decisions and experiments for improvement the next year. Final exam data in PLC discussion looks something like the following. Which group of students achieved mastery, and which did not? Why? Identify improvement in populations and compare changes made throughout the year. Is there a correlation? What questions did student miss most often, and what skill mistakes did they make? Why? Hypothesize changes for next year to directly address the data. What patterns did you observe in student performance throughout the year, and how did it impact the final exam and/or lab practicum?

As for the second goal in my classroom, that students will have a positive experience in chemistry, a Likert scale survey provides the measure. In administering the survey, I politely request the students be honest but kind. They communicate mostly in kindness, although I've learned through experience not to take things personally. All teachers in the PLC administer the survey and share results. Practicing a blame-free culture and remembering these are teenagers, we academically evaluate student responses together in an emotionally safe and supportive space. I gain huge insight from how another teacher interprets what students say about my classroom. The survey includes questions about what the students liked and disliked about the class. What resource(s) most helped them learn? During the class period, what one thing was most beneficial in producing understanding? What is the one thing they would change in the classroom? What would improve the learning experience? Did they feel safe, respected, cared for? Most of the questions contain a list to choose from as well as an open-response option. Without a doubt, some of the best ideas we implemented as a PLC over the years were derived from the student Likert survey.

When creating your measure, consider the following items.

- Make it quantifiable. You must look at numbers!
- Make it trackable. Keep data from year to year.
- Use the SMART Goal model:
    o Specific
    o Measurable
    o Attainable
    o Relevant
    o Time-Based

When evaluating the data from the measure, ask two questions. Where is there improvement? What needs improvement? The measure builds in the feedback loop tying everything together. We work hard to remove waste and improve processes, so students have the ultimate learning experience in our classroom. The measure quantifiably shows if we achieved the goal and where we need to improve moving forward.

I teach lab-based STEM (Science, Technology, Engineering, and Mathematics) content, and my measure accurately reflects the setting. The measure, however, is not limited to a multiple-choice test and lab practicum. Measure examples include essay, short-response, project, group project, oral report, presentation, research, video, and interview to name a few. You are the expert in your classroom and know best what type of measure appropriately reflects your goal.

An added benefit of the measure comes in the form of influence. Numbers prompt change and inspire action. Do you need money for your classroom or resources to support your teaching efforts? Use data! Data acts like ammunition to get the ball rolling in a classroom, PLC, department, or school. Maybe you want to make a change in your classroom that is experimental or deviates from usual school practice. Use data to get permission to change. Numbers talk, souse your numbers to secure resources and permission to increase value in your classroom.

Remember the principle Define: Customer, Goal, Measure. Numerous times, in my early years of utilizing Lean, I approached my husband asking his opinion about something in my classroom. He always responded with, "Does it add value for your customer to achieve the goal as revealed in your measure?" As a PLC, when we hit a wall, we always retrace our steps back to who our customer is, what our goal is, and how do we measure the goal? The foundation of defining our customer (student), goal (student learning), and measure (quantitative), acts like a target to determine what we do or do not do. If XYZ does not add value to the student learning as reflected in the measure, then it is waste and we do not do it! Again, keep the customer, goal, and measure in front of you with laser focus. These definitions give you the framework to answer almost all questions quickly and easily as you move through Lean Think.

Chapter 3: Mindset

Dr. Carol Dweck, author of the groundbreaking book, *Mindset: The New Psychology of Success*, says, "Becoming is better than being" (2017). We all walk a path, and Lean Think affords the mindset to intentionally "become" better through process improvement. In this journey, three states exist in the process: Current state, Future State, and Improvement State. The current state identifies where I am right now, the future state shows where I want to be, and the improvement state moves me from where I am to where I want to be.

Where Am I?

The current state evaluates where a classroom is right now. This possibly conjures feelings of disappointment or criticism. Stop that train right now! Identifying the state of a classroom, honestly, happens in a blame-free zone. Soon to be equipped with tools to do things better, classrooms are "becoming." Classifying the current state simply marks the starting line without judgment or condemnation.

To ascertain a classroom's current state, observe it. Sit back and watch the students. Survey movement and participation. Listen to conversation, questions, and statements. Time activities for mobilization and completion. Get a sense of the feeling in the classroom; make mental notes of facial expressions, i.e., smiles, frowns, quizzical brows, timidity, freedom, respect, withdrawn looks. Scrutinize student behavior between students themselves and between students and adults.

As discussed earlier, the primary product of every classroom is student learning. Pull up data and candidly summarize the numbers. Where are the students in relationship to the classroom goal? Sometimes teachers brush aside data with excuses such as: The second-grade teachers did not teach the foundations well, so now I pay the price as the third-grade teacher; the fifth-grade test is harder than the end-of-year fourth grade test; there are so many IEPs in my classroom; junior high did not prepare the students for the rigors of high school, etc. Remove all exceptions and factually appraise student performance.

Teachers also need to take a self-assessment of how they feel and mentally record what they do throughout the day. Rate job satisfaction based on peace of mind and enjoyment. Ask, "How do I feel at the end of the day? Contentment, satisfaction, peace, exhaustion, dread, discouragement?" Estimate the amount of time worked every day, every week. Probe what takes the most time or what creates points of irritation during the day.

Reviewing student performance qualitatively and quantitatively gives a strong overview of the current state from the customer's perspective. Teachers factoring in their emotions, effort, time, and enjoyment complete the picture for the classroom's current state. Sincerely pinpointing recent practices and achievements is the first step in successfully moving toward the future state.

Utopia

I jokingly quip the future state is where angels sing and all things harmonize perfectly. If everything in the classroom reached perfection, what would it look like? Consider the observations, data, and feelings uncovered in the current state, and hold them up against a flawless image of an ideal classroom. Try this: Close your eyes and visualize your ideal classroom. What are the students doing (or not doing)? What does the classroom look like? What are you doing (or not doing)? For a moment, assess how you feel. Imagine how your students feel in your classroom. Predict student learning and data from student performance in that classroom, and you've found the future state.

As a little girl, I spread my arms out as far as possible and told my mom I loved her "this much!" She then stretched her longer arms out to her sides and joyfully exclaimed, "But I love you this much!" She then scooped me in her arms with a giant hug — such a sweet memory. Now envision your arms reaching to each side from your body. Remember how the left hand represents the current state, and the right hand represents the future state. The chasm existing between your two hands is no problem, because the gap closes as you begin the improvement state. Every day you implement Lean Think principles, the left hand moves closer and closer to the right hand; the current state becomes more like the future state.

Does This Add Value?

The improvement state is where teachers live and work. The seminal question, "Does this add value?" represents the heart of Lean Think. I asked my husband a thousand times for advice and a thousand times he replied with a very kind, "Does it add value?" I was slow to learn, but with enough Pavlovian conditioning, I now consistently apply the same question in every aspect of life.

The main takeaway of the book is to ask the question, "DOES THIS ADD VALUE?" Let it become a habit, second nature. For every question, idea, proposal, change, or innovation that comes to mind, employ the question, "Does this add value?" This question provides a filter. It is the medieval watchman standing guard, judging what passes through the gate and enters the keep. The question determines what items or actions qualify as waste or value and, consequentially, which are removed and/or engaged.

To drive this home, do a visualization exercise. The set parameters, the customer, the goal, and the measure stand in front of you like a target, and the current and future states flank your sides. The current and future states represent the incremental process improvement of moving from where you are to where you want to be. The target, students accomplishing the classroom goal as shown by the measure, directs the daily decisions you make to succeed in this endeavor.

Now, imagine placing a rectangular filter between you and the target. I picture a thin, metal handheld mirror with no mirror; you see through the metal frame and only certain items can pass through this filter. (See Chapter 1 Diagram.) That filter, the gatekeeper, is the question, "Does this add value?" As an idea percolates in your brain, apply the filter. Does this idea add value to my student achieving the goal as reflected in the measure? If it adds value, then the idea passes through the filter and you implement it. If the idea lacks value, then you throw it out as waste. You only keep items or do activities that ADD VALUE to your customer to accomplish the goal as confirmed by the measure!

What Is Value?

In industry, the needs of the customer determine value. If a customer desires a sunroof in a new car, a manufacturer will add a sunroof to the car. That sunroof, therefore, adds value to the car. If a car consumer feels indifferent about a blinking light on the door handle, the manufacturer will not install a blinking light on the door handle. That falls in the category of waste because it does not add value to the product the customer wants.

Value in education differs ever so slightly. Something only adds value to a student if it produces student learning. Period. The deviation from industry comes from the fact that students do not wholly define what is valuable for them. If young students solely defined value at school, recess would comprise 6 of the 7 school hours with one happy hour for lunch. Educational customers, being minors, need help defining value, so teachers gladly share the burden of defining value in the classroom.

Lean Manufacturing utilizes three criteria to define "Value" within the context of process improvement. Although the criteria lack

100% overlap with education, they still provide useful tools in fleshing out what passes through an academic filter as valuable.

- The customer is willing to pay for the product.
- Any given action in the process must change the product.
- An individual step must be done correctly the first time.

Criterion 1: How does the idea of payment work with education? While speaking at a Lean Think workshop several years ago, a young elementary teacher raised her hand and said, "I don't think parents would pay me to play Reading Rainbow videos for their children." This is an important observation because parents and students don't pay for the product directly, thus amending this part of Value. But ask: If a parent paid for services rendered, would they pay for activities observed in your classroom? Attach a dollar sign to each activity in your classroom and assess whether or not it adds value. If not, get rid of it.

Criterion 2: Ideally, every moment in a classroom moves students through the learning process. Every second should *change* their academic experience in a positive, forward motion. But does this happen in actuality? Big fat no. When you honestly assess how many minutes during a class period are changing/improving student learning, you quickly realize that the percentage is low. Enter the idea of value. When determining if something adds value to the student and their learning experience, evaluate how much of the activity actually increases their learning experience. Then decide whether to keep it or change it.

Criterion 3: Every step in the process must be done right the first time. This does not mean students learn something with one explanation. We chuckle at the thought. For example, brain theory suggests it takes at least 10 impressions (learning experiences) for a student to commit understanding to long-term memory. So, teachers plan accordingly and design lessons with 10 or more learning repetitions. Value presents itself when each step in the process or plan is executed as intended to accomplish a given purpose.

Poll students and ask what they deem valuable in education. Answers will generally fall into 1 of 3 categories: needs, wants, and desires. With regard to *needs*, all students require safe, inviting schools and classrooms. No one can learn unless they feel protected. Some students need additional resources like food or mental health assistance just to enable them to learn.

Next, the majority of students identify they *want* to learn. Just as teachers dislike waste, students also do not want to waste their time sitting in a classroom doing nothing. Students want to learn and be equipped for success in life.

Finally, student *desires* can be described as "delighters." These are the experiences that send stars dancing through their hearts and minds. For example, moments of inspiration, victory over challenge, creativity displayed, perfection nailed in performance, and awe through discovery all fuel delight in their school experience. Oh, the joy as an educator to help a student feel delight and wonder in learning. To judge if something in a classroom adds value, juxtapose a student's needs, wants, and desires. If it contributes to student learning in the context of those three things, then it can pass through the filter.

Using the Filter: An Example

I began my chemistry PLC's journey by asking the pivotal question, "Does this add value?" In 2015, all the chemistry teachers pulled out, collectively, 50 years' worth of stuff. Favorite labs, handmade assignments, proven demos, beloved activities, and weathered exams sat in front of us. Over the course of nine teaching months, we left no stone unturned. We touched everything we did or made our students do and asked, "Does this add value?" In the first year implementing Lean Think, our singular objective was to remove waste. No matter how emotionally attached we were to the item, if it did not add value to students learning chemistry as measured by the SAGE test, we threw it out. Piles and piles of previous years' learning tools (that no longer (or ever) added value) littered our trash cans.

By removing waste and only focusing on what added value for our students to learn chemistry according to the end-of-year exam, thanks to the filter, general chemistry students increased from 37% to 56% proficiency. The entire chemistry PLC, including all chemistry students, increased from 63% to 69% proficiency. Notice, we did not do anything new! We just got rid of ineffective exercises and focused on the things that truly added value to students learning chemistry.

Look closely at the mechanism for improvement. With sharpshooter focus, we set the target. The exclusive *customer*, the student, was assigned the *goal* of learning chemistry, which was assessed by the SAGE exam, the *measure*. We placed the powerful filter, "Does this add value?" between the target and our 50 years of stuff. As we touched each item and asked, "Does this add value?" it became clear which items added value and which did not, and we kept or threw them out accordingly.

Ninety percent of the time, we knew to keep or throw something away in a fraction of a second. The other 10% of the time, discussion ensued, which always circled back to who the customer is, what the goal is, and how we measure the goal. Looking intently at the definitions set for the class, with the backdrop of the value filter, we consistently came to consensus. In all our discussion and massive waste removal that first Lean Think year, only two items survived as an exception and did not fulfill the customer, goal, and measure parameters. They are mentioned later in the book.

It is imperative to set the customer, goal and measure for your classroom, PLC, department, school, and district. Without these as your target, the filter fails to work. Asking, "Does this add value?" only applies if there is something to add value to — the target. Additionally, as work begins, the target should always ground the discussion. As questions arise, go back to the customer, goal, and measure. Fixed marks make easier targets, so fix your customer, goal, and measure to make it easier to determine if items add value.

Kaizen

Everything shared thus far in the book is a beautiful example of *kaizen*, or change for the better. Two Japanese kanji characters form kaizen: *kai* meaning change, and *zen* meaning good. Together they translate to mean improvement, or continuous improvement. Industry adopted the term, kaizen, to embody the continuous, incremental improvement ideology. In application, select one step in a process and work to improve it by removing waste or increasing effectiveness and efficiency.

My PLC's initial kaizen project simply required one action which produced one of two possible outcomes. We asked the question, "Does this add value?" of every action and item in our classrooms, and based on our answer, we either kept it or discarded it. Most seasoned teachers begin with this same kaizen project. New teachers begin kaizen with load-leveling (Chapter 13).

Incremental process improvement is not only for large projects. Everyone uses kaizen, whether they know it or not, every day and everywhere. For example, moving a squinting student closer to the board, reviewing a test question all students missed, or placing a pie tin under the hand sanitizer so it does not drip on the floor all show process improvements. Every day we probe what adds value and how we can do better. It is truly a mindset of "becoming," just like Dr. Dweck's book describes, and several strategies can set the stage for a kaizen mindset.

Brainstorming ideas to achieve the ideal future state without ridicule of self or others is crucial. I like to think of this strategy as turning over a rock. Recently, I threw away a broken steppingstone from my garden. Picture what I unearthed as I pried the stone from the dirt; worms and potato bugs scurried through tunnels to escape the sunlight. I experienced a new sight in comparison to the butterfly-etched stone. Similarly, turn over a rock in teaching practices. Can this be done a different way? If I can only use technology, how could I teach this? If I had no technology, what resources could I use? As quickly as possible, list three ways a topic can be taught differently.

Challenge the status quo. The quintessential mindset to battle is "This is how it has always been done." Kill that statement. This does not imply that things done in the past are not valuable. Instead, it removes the unwillingness to try something new and empowers change. Push the status quo. What has been done the same forever, year in and year out? Look at steps in processes of grandfathered events. Where can waste be removed? Where can improvement be added through technology and updated questions or supplementing with current news?

Find the most simple, flexible, and smallest solution. I tell a story at workshops how the Fischer Pen Company invested $1 million to invent a space pen workable in zero gravity (*History of Space Pens*, 2021). American astronauts use the space pen. By contrast, Russian astronauts use a 10-cent pencil. Did the million-dollar space pen add any more value than the pencil? Doubtful.

The point of all this is just because something is elaborate or expensive does not mean it adds value. Teachers erroneously think if the project is bigger, they put in more time, students work harder, and they spend more, then the students learn more. This is unequivocally false. More does not mean better or valuable. In contrast, the fewer resources something requires to add the same amount of value, the better. I learned early in my career that if students show proficiency by completing five homework problems, then I do not give them 10 problems. If students master a lab technique in parts A-C, then they do not do part D. Likewise, when problem-solving for classroom systems, always look for the fastest, easiest solution that adds value. While it seems counterintuitive to our habits, the faster and easier the solution, the more value it offers. Fewer moving parts means less can go wrong. Keep it simple!

Watch processes in your classroom. Observe students and the teacher to reveal kaizen opportunities. Intentionally survey and listen to students. Take notes during the observation. Video the classroom and examine both the teacher's and students' movement, actions, attention, and words. Time student and teacher activities. How long does it take students to get out technology, turn in papers, mobilize to rotations? How long does it take a teacher to grade math tests? Measure physical and academic steps. How many steps do students take to get to the supply station? How many steps to move to essay stations? How many times is that one item touched and by how many students? How often does a teacher reach for the same item? How many questions did students ask before they began the art project? How many students required rework? Scrutinize real time processes and discover kaizen goldmines.

Most importantly, be emboldened. YOU (the teacher) are the expert in your classroom. You have an intimate understanding of your strengths, content, grade level, administration, resources, and demographic unlike any other person on the planet. If a change is going to be made, you are absolutely the BEST person to make that change in your classroom.

Think about a worker standing in an assembly line deftly attaching widget A to widget B. If a change needs to be made to this portion of the assembly line, the accountant on the third floor, stockholder, CEO, or lineman manager do not know the best solution to make changes in widgets A and B. They all go to the expert, the boots on the ground, the soldier in the trenches … the worker who has attached thousands of widgets A to widgets B. The soldier in the educational trenches is you, the teacher!

When a teacher takes ownership as the expert, a powerful transformation occurs. The teacher begins leading the administration and direction of the school, and rightly so. Teachers are closest to the customer, the student. Teachers work directly with the customer and are the expert in the customer's needs, wants, and desires. Changes in school goals, district policy, state curriculum, and legislative mandates should come from teachers … because they know the customer best.

This year our AP World History teacher taught one credit recovery class (alternate class where students redo failed coursework to earn graduation credit). Everything this woman touches turns to gold. She told me part of her soul died each time she watched these dejected students sit at a computer to work through meaningless modules while hating everything about life and school. As an expert teacher, she proposed a change to both the school and district. Wise administrators and district directors stepped aside and gave her the green light. They were wise: Let the expert work and see value increase for students in their learning experience.

This is the process of *becoming* the best possible teacher to enable students to experience optimum learning, all within contract time.

Chapter 4: Let's Get Organized

The first three steps in 6S get things organized while the last three steps keep things organized. Let's focus on the first three: Sort, Straighten, and Scrub.

At the conclusion of a Lean Think workshop several years ago, a veteran teacher of 35 years approached me with a gleam in her eye. She shared how liberated she felt when she realized she didn't have to keep everything! Come to find out, she still housed material from her student teaching days three and a half decades prior. She flatly told me, "I thought I had to keep everything." That same afternoon, her principal texted pictures of boxes and boxes she had stacked outside her classroom marked for disposal. Everyone rejoiced.

A favorite of teachers, 6S describes the organization mechanism in Lean. It simply stands for 6 words that begin with the letter S and are meant to be followed sequentially (sounds like a teacher's trick):

- Sort
- Straighten
- Scrub
- Systemize
- Standardize
- Safety

Many teachers discover they've already completed a couple of steps in their classroom. Just begin the list where it fits.

Sort

Two summers ago, I completed a major sort in my house. I set the timer for one hour every day for the month of July. With a mixture of trepidation and excitement, I literally touched everything in my house to determine if it added value. You can imagine what I found: tarragon spice from my sweet mother-in-law that expired 17 years ago, hot rollers unused since high school, 25-year-old wedding cards sitting in a box. The best was my kindergarten report card from second term. The teacher said I was coming along, recognizing the sound and shape of all the letters of the alphabet, except for the letter J. My name is Julie. Lord bless teachers. I kept the report card and got rid of everything else.

In the sort stage, everything falls into one of three categories: keep, give away, or throw away. To know which category an item falls, apply the filter. Ask, "Does this add value?" Completing a sort in my classroom three times within a 10-year span, I kept asking, "Does this add value for my students to learn chemistry as reflected on the end of year test?" If an item adds value to a student's learning experience, place it to the *Keep* pile. If the item does not add value in your classroom, could it be valuable to someone else? If so, set it in the *Give Away* pile. If the item does not add value to you or anyone else, *Throw it away*.

What is the challenge in this step? All teachers have said, "I might need this." Fear of throwing something away and requiring it down the road forces educators to stuff more into the filing cabinet and balance another box in the cupboard. Effectiveness in Sorting comes with a paradigm shift. First, imagine a teacher needs to create a new resource. The majority of the time, what is the first response? Look on the internet! Teachers rarely peruse old paper files or search messy computer files. They type the topic in a search bar to access current, relevant resources.

I understand the energy and personal investment in making a resource and using it, and then setting it aside for a future use. It's difficult to let go of what I have made, so my cupboards and cabinets are overstocked with items I never use. To avoid this, make one master file of originals. For items that may genuinely be useful in the future, keep one copy either in a physical master file or as an electronic copy on the computer in a folder titled "Keep." Recycle or delete extra copies. I go through the master file once a year in the spring. If five years pass without using a resource, I discard it. Honestly, most temporarily retired items remain unused as the need for new resources requires ... new resources.

A second thought overcomes the fear of getting rid of stuff: I can replace something if needed. When I purged my house, that mindset helped. Over the course of a month, I filled our third-car garage parking space three times with giveaway piles. I discarded thousands of items. In giving away so much, I inevitably knew I would regret a couple of my decisions. However, the loss of two items I would have to purchase for $20 was 100% worth it for the benefit of decluttering my home and mind.

After that house cleansing in July, sure enough, nine months later I needed cowboy boots and a hat for a school assembly. (I embarrassingly danced in front of the student body. Oh, the things teachers agree to do!) I had given both of mine away because they sat unused in my closet for 20 years. No worries, I wore pseudo-cowboy boots and borrowed my husband's cowboy hat. Believe me, no one looked at my wannabe boots or marginally oversized hat as students roared with laughter at my dance.

Through three classroom purges over 10 years, only one person wanted something I had put into the dumpster, a dusty wedding cake made with three tiers of toilet paper and silk flowers. A physics teacher asked to please use the wedding monstrosity to demonstrate the marriage between nonmetals sharing electrons. Fortunately, the instructor chose to illustrate covalent bonding another way. The point here is that you will only regret one or two decisions. Count it as the worthwhile price of removing hundreds or thousands of items that do not add value. If you go into the process knowing you will get rid of something that will only cost a small amount to replace, then decluttering the classroom is that much easier.

I applied a five-year rule to give away unused items. The popular book, *The Life-Changing Magic of Tidying Up* by Mari Kondo, tells readers to discard items if unused within one year (2014). I struggle to get rid of resources after only one year, but that's my own weakness. Five years, though, feels doable. Everyone may have a slightly different threshold, but 35 years does not count! Make it less than seven years at most.

What to do with items generously given or bequeathed to you presents another challenge when decluttering. But apply the same filter and approach. Ask, "Does this add value in my classroom?" and "How long has it sat on the shelf?" If needed, take a picture to remember a kindness or add a copy to your master file. Then pass it on or throw it away. In my first declutter, I threw away microfiche (old-school friend of researchers), recycled 50-year-old books, discarded broken glassware, and safely disposed inappropriate high school chemicals. The retiring teacher who conferred his 30-year teaching collection and room to me, generously left *everything*. Moving the classroom into a new century meant sifting through equipment and resources to find and keep what truly added value. Clearing out the items was not a personal assessment or indictment of the previous teacher; it merely updated the classroom for the benefit of the students according to my teaching style.

Giving and throwing away unnecessary items not only creates space in cabinets and files but also in a person's mind. Right now, think of where you last put the fingernail clippers. Do you have a clothespin somewhere in your classroom or house? How about miscellaneous screws or a flathead screwdriver? Your favorite yardstick? Items occupy physical, electronic, and *mental* space.

Remove the waste and the space can be utilized for useful purposes.

Straighten

Looking at the beloved *keep* pile, the million-dollar question becomes, "Where do I put it all now?" My husband's office disintegrates in this step. Sure, he gives and throws away, but then he looks at the piles left over and is lost as to where to put things. *Straighten*, the second step in 6S, presents the solution. Follow this motto: Find a place for everything and put everything in its place. Find a strategic home for individual items and consistently deposit them back in their home after use.

To begin, look at each item and decide if it's used regularly or occasionally. For regular use items, keep them close to or where they are used. Occasional use items go in cupboards or drawers at a distance from everyday activity. For example, I use my stapler daily, so it sits on the right side of my desk. In contrast, I only employ my three-hole punch a couple of times a month. The stylish, lime green hole punch is therefore tucked into my top right desk drawer, out of sight and away from desk traffic yet accessible enough to grab without walking for it. Even more removed are extra manila and green hanging file folders in boxes behind the whiteboard. Why? Because I pull those out only once a year to create new student files.

Four straightening hacks can help you find a place for everything, whether used daily or infrequently. First, establish and delineate a standard place for each item. As you begin putting things away from the sort experience, avoid the temptation to place something "temporarily in this spot." Months later, it's no surprise the item never fully garnered a permanent place, physically or in my head. In the straighten stage, determine to strategically secure a final spot for each item. Do not set anything down until you find its intentional new home.

Second, let usage frequency and location guide your decisions. As mentioned before, put things used frequently close to the area they employ or where they are handled most. Put items used infrequently further from everyday transactions. The idea is for students and teachers to take as few steps as possible to access supplies. For instance, students use staplers in both my classroom and lab daily. I've purposely placed four baskets with staplers in my teaching space, two in the classroom by student folders and two in the lab near supply stations. As a result, students never have to "go get" a stapler. When they think, "I need a stapler," voila! The stapler just happens to be at the right place at the right time.

To further streamline usage and frequency, consider housing groups of items as families. If the teacher or students repeatedly utilize the same items in a given situation, store them as a group. Perhaps each student table uses crayons, glue sticks, pencils, and stapler daily. Make baskets to house all the objects together to accommodate students. In my case, on two shelves in the back north corner of my room rest boxes of individual demo and lab families. Rather than collect equipment and supplies from all over the room each time I do a particular demo or lab, I simply pull out one box that contains most everything I need for a certain lab or demo. This does not work for all demos and labs but for many. For those science teachers reading, no worries, all chemicals are safely stored in their designated Flinn areas!

Lastly, a straighten hack I discovered in my classroom revealed the need for EMPTY SPACE. Do not fill cupboards, files, drawers, and closets to the brim. You need wiggle room to quickly put something away without sliding, lifting, scooting, or balancing other items. During a follow-up elementary school visit, a librarian poignantly illustrated this point. She stored games in her back office for students to play once they completed reading activities. She told me the organization of the games looked like a Jenga contraption. Only the librarian accessed and put away the games because only she knew how everything perfectly fit into the single cabinet. It required her time and energy managing the games for each class.

In her straighten step, she revolutionized the process. She cleared a cupboard within the main library and only put half the games on it. She LEFT SPACE for different arrangements of games to still fit neatly in the cupboard. Students now get out and put away their own games. With plenty of room to house the games, the students do not have to follow an elaborate and precise pattern of placement. The games sit neatly but uniquely for each class rotation. The librarian rotates the games from her cabinet to the library cabinet periodically. This saves them all time, gives students responsibility, and easily keeps the library tidy.

As with anything in Lean, you can apply process improvement to the straighten step. Deliberately choose a home for each item based on usage and frequency. Then try it out. Once everything is set, let it marinate for a while. Experience and observe the flow and accessibility of items. After you experience the new arrangement, make tweaks and adjustments accordingly to continually improve its value. The straighten step represents an initial, intentional effort to place things in an optimum area to add the most value for users. Only after living in the space will the necessary changes surface. Feel at liberty to make those adjustments to improve organization.

Scrub

I breathe gratification after delving into a good scrub, removing all the dust crumbs and spots blanketing shelves. Intuitively, people working in a clean area tend to be more positive and productive. Students attending an orderly school have more respect for themselves and their education. The same applies to classrooms or homes. Surrounding ourselves with clutter, filth, and mess can foster a cluttered, filthy, and messy mindset. A clean and polished living space fosters a clean and polished mindset.

Choose from two approaches for the scrub step. Some prefer to put on yellow gloves and tie back their hair after the sort and straighten steps are complete. The scrub motion sweeps through every inch of space to make it shine from a deep scouring. This is the first option, but I favor the second approach: I complete the scrub step *while* I sort and straighten. Because everything is already pulled out of shelves, as I decide what to keep and where things go, I wipe down cupboards and vacuum drawers as a I proceed. When I assign a new home to an object, I then place it on a gleaming surface. After checking off the straighten step, very few areas remain to finish during the last bit of scrub, leaving the place sparkling.

Trial and error occur in the organization process as some missteps surface over time. But remember, overall, feel emboldened and empowered to remove waste and only keep what adds value to you and your students as you get organized.

Chapter 5: Keep the 6S Going

The next two steps in 6S keep things organized, something most teachers struggle to do day in and day out. Yet if they systemize and standardize, then classroom efficiency continually improves along with student learning.

Systemize

Several of my daughters fall apart at this step. They will perfect their room, clean it with a fine-tooth comb so nothing exists under their beds and the clothes are hanging color-coded by group. It is a wondrous site. However, within two days DEFCON alarms blare as clothes cover the carpet, books fill corners, and garbage overflows. The fourth step, systemize, provides the mechanism to avoid this kind of breakdown and keep things tidy.

The driving principle behind systemize is to simply put things back when finished using them. Make it both a personal and classroom rule that after using something, it immediately goes back to its designated place in perfect condition. This means refilling an empty bottle or stapler before returned, noting a needed purchase on a running "to buy" list, or wiping off drips, smudges, and spills. Restored to perfect condition, an item is then placed exactly where it belongs.

Labeling or color coding easily helps students put things back in correct places. Make it visual. I say "6S it!" The manufacturing industry skillfully applies visual cues to maintain a tidy environment. Visit a manufacturing company and notice the yellow stripes on the floor indicating where to walk. Tool walls have foam cutouts for individual tools, so wrenches, hammers, and sockets only fit in one spot. Black tape on the floor outlines exactly where to set buckets.

I employed 6S manufacturing practices in my lab. Two sophisticated Ohaus analytical scales sit on my back lab bench. Understandably, you're envious of how the 100.000 g balance reads to the thousandth place. They are awesome. Every time they are moved, I must relevel them because of their high sensitivity. The word "I" is really code for my husband. He relevels them for me. I usually bribe him with food and a smile. In years past, I told my students to not move the scales because my husband would catch on to the bribery, calculate that the food is not worth his effort, and then I would be stuck releveling the scales. Even with that story, students still slid the scales to make room for bustling lab activities. This happened repeatedly until it got 6S-ed. One time after my kind husband leveled both scales, he put baby blue tape against the black countertop precisely in the base shape of each scale. Since that time, I tell the same story to each class, and the scales have not moved in years. Simply outlining the scales with tape communicates to the students, "Wait! The scales belong here. DO NOT move them."

In your classroom, do the students always struggle to find the stapler and ask you where it is? Does Table 4 consistently misplace the bench supply basket? Are computer chairs on the opposite side of the room, not even close to the desktops? 6S it! Put tape on the table around the stapler. When a student uses the stapler, it goes back inside the tape rectangle. Mark each table with bright yellow tape in the shape of a square, exactly where you want the supply basket to rest. Put tape on the floor for each desktop chair. When they are finished with the desktop, students slide the chairs until they fit within the lines.

In a similar hack example, a seventh-grade science teacher experienced remarkable success after color-coding her class. Each of six classroom benches displayed color labels. She also numbered each chair around the tables, 1-6. At times, different lab supplies sat on different benches, but the color of tape on supplies matched the color of the bench where they belonged. As a result, students quickly knew where to return supplies. Student folders also matched the colored benches. Lab notebooks lived in the same color folder as the classroom bench where the students sat. When the teacher rapidly gave instructions using color/number prompts, students responded without question: Yellow bench begin rotation one, red bench write the prelab in your lab notebook, all number 2 students gather your table's starters and place them in the green bench basket for group grading. The tool of color-coding and numbering created a highly understandable and efficient system of organization in her room.

Even with a commitment to always put things back correctly and in perfect condition, a routine of consistent tidying is necessary. Write down your routine and calendar it. Include a daily, weekly, quarterly, yearly, and if necessary, activity routine. My daily minimum routine is to simply leave my desk clean at the end of the day. If a pile of to-do papers still sit on my desk, they lie in the to-do pile neatly. For my weekly routine, I chose Friday as my day to sweep through the classroom and lab. It typically takes five minutes or less. Quarterly, I let students work off low citizenship marks by cleaning. They scrub sinks, wipe counters, dust, and straighten cupboards. Yearly, in May, I do a spring-cleaning. I go through every cupboard, closet, and drawer to make sure everything has a place, and everything is in its place. I purge files physically and electronically. The cherry on top comes from placing an equipment order for the next year. Because spring-cleaning helps hone the ongoing "to buy" list, I create a solid purchase list in preparation for the fall.

Students daily engage the systemize routine. When activities transpire in the classroom, no one is released until everything is put away correctly and things are tidy. In fact, in labs, students watch me inspect their lab station to receive a 10-point clean-up mark before they are excused. Fifteen seconds before the bell rings, I ask students to straighten their desks, slide books neatly into the desk tray, and pick up trash.

To maintain the strong sort, straighten, and scrub you've already established through time, sweat, and thought, write maintenance routines and calendar them. Make students a part of the upkeep. With consistent habits and schedules, the system of preserving cleanliness and order works effectively.

Standardize

Standardize simply means 6S organization practices become the expectation and habit. Standardization always flows from the teacher. As with any classroom experience, students adopt patterns through consistent classroom procedures, repeated cues, and reiterated positive benchmarks.

Just because the system and mindset of 6S establishes practices, this does not mean the standards are immovable or inflexible. Education is fluid; it changes with the ebb and flow of student population, cultural norms, technology impact, and administrative styles. Standardization provides a solid foundation fostering a highly functional classroom that adjusts to outside changes through incremental process improvement.

Watch processes and assess their effectiveness. A process with this year's classroom demographic may not be as effective with next year's student group. Feel free to experiment and change. Most standards cross-apply seamlessly from class to class. For the few practices that don't function as well in new settings, adjust them. That is the power of Lean and incremental process improvement. Get organized, create a system to stay organized, then make minor tweaks along the way. Make this your expectation and habit.

A Word About Electronic Organization

Most examples given for the first five steps in 6S illustrate physical organization. 6S also applies to electronic storage. Move through the same sequence to spruce up a laptop, desktop, or mobile device. Choose an evening, put on a favorite movie, and sort. Delete every unneeded file, app, and program. Then create folders and straighten by moving files into folders. Clear up display screens by moving icons into a cloud or folder. To Scrub, perform a defrag when finished or invest in a clean-up program. Once a year, at the end of school, follow the same pattern and your electronic space remains nice and tidy.

Overview

Sort, straighten, scrub, systemize, and standardize, five simple words that can create life-changing practices. Because life is life, periodically circle back through the steps in the process. For example, after nine years of teaching, I felt inspired to begin afresh with sort. It only took four hours as compared to 40 the first time I did it. Amazingly, I still gave and threw away boxes of bits and bobs. With an observant eye, teachers know when to revisit a step. Just as a reminder, do not let things slide. The moment a teacher sees something needing attention, that is the moment to intervene. Otherwise, organization quickly spirals into chaos. Yes, this is experience talking.

Lean originally stopped at 5S. Not until recently did manufacturing add the sixth S, safety. The first five steps address surrounding order, placement, and usefulness of things that the worker and customer access. Because workspaces inherently impact people, organization, efficiency, and quality. The most significant impact of a clean and tidy surrounding, however, is the safety of the worker and customer, 6S.

Chapter 6: Safety

It took several years for me to figure out how the sixth S, safety, fit into the educational application of Lean. Do we coach kids how not to staple fingers? Teaching a lab-based class, I absolutely understand the value of instructing my students in laboratory safety protocols. But what about math and English classes? Elementary and middle school students? Tell students not to eat crayons? Sure, education teaches kids how to avoid strangers, live healthy lifestyles, avoid substance abuse, etc. But what about safety in the actual classroom?

The answer hit like a ton of bricks while sitting with a group of third-grade teachers. I took a personal day, leaving my students to take a test with a substitute teacher, to do a Lean Think follow-up with two elementary schools. Visiting a nearby elementary school, I observed classrooms, then sat for 15 minutes with each grade PLC during their preps to answer questions and get feedback. Positioned around a circular table, four of the five third-grade teachers discussed traditional versus open classroom designs when the fifth teacher joined us. A darling, experienced yet younger educator sat quietly with tears rolling down her cheeks. The administrative intern had just helped her remove a student from her class and remained behind to monitor the young man in the office while waiting for a parent to pick him up. She then recounted how this student began overturning desks and yelling at the students in the class. Once she got the classroom under control, another student approached saying she was afraid the boy would begin throwing his shoes at the class. Come to find out, a form of this outburst happened … every day. Exhausted and defeated, her shoulders sagged as the tears silently flowed for the next 15 minutes. At that moment, I understood safety in education; every teacher and student must feel and be safe at school at every moment, with every person, in every space. Look at the impact of that one child's outburst. Clearly the child acting out most likely battled insecurities in other areas of his life. The teacher obviously had been violated. What about the other 25 children in the classroom? Undoubtedly, each had fearful, defensive mechanisms engaged. As administration intervened, fellow teachers observed the aftermath, and parents had to pick up the pieces. All involved had unsettled nerves, probing questions, and deep concern. The incident touched a significant number of people in profound ways.

With classroom safety defined, I began copious research reading numerous articles and books, and I interviewed administrators, educators, and counselors. I am by no means an expert on all the areas within education safety. However, what I found is enlightening and led me to other resources for additional support as follows.

Most intriguing in my research is 60% of all teachers I polled claim students have fundamentally changed over the years. Teachers say behavioral norms and the overall classroom dynamic has altered from as little as 10-15 years ago. I showed this data to one of my former vice principals, whom I greatly respect. Having spent 30 years working in both public and private sectors of mental health, his expertise in Special Education provides great wisdom. He claims students have not fundamentally changed, but life issues have cycled to children at younger ages than a decade ago. For example, extreme anxiety and suicide were rarely elementary school concerns in the early 2000s. Now they are common concerns with third to sixth graders.

The pressing question is why? Why the change, why the shift? Unfortunately, academic literature presents myriad ideas, many of which are contradictory. For every idea I researched, I found both positive and negative evidence: It is diet, it is not diet; parenting is more progressive, parenting is more traditional; the society's moral revolution has an impact, society's moral adjustments have no impact. Flip a coin! The elephant in the room, of course, is social media. Most literature points to the unintended negative impacts of social media. Yet, there is no shortage of research strongly supporting constructive aspects of social media. The sum of the research is inconclusive; academia cannot pinpoint a root cause for the changes seen in school age children within the last two decades. However, experts present solid strategies to effectively work with difficult children and situations.

I do not profess to be an authority on trauma or mental health issues. What follows is a conglomeration of many books, articles, and interviews to identify tools for teachers to utilize when working with difficult children. It outlines classroom management resources, the pattern to use when working with a difficult student, a list of go-to affirmative behavior tools, and where to solicit help beyond the teacher.

Classroom Management

Every teacher begins with classroom management. Regardless of the content, grade level, or demographic, foundational to learning is classroom management. Providing a safe, predictable, orderly environment where all participants follow the same social norms and expectations enables student learning. Before a teacher can begin teaching, classroom management must be established. Without it, instruction is ineffective, and students will not learn. The absolute best resource I found on the topic is Harry K. Wong and Rosemary T. Wong's *The First Days of School: How to be an Effective Teacher* (1997). I read this book every August before school begins. If your classroom management needs a tune up or you are in the throes of creating healthy rules and expectations, jump into this book. Once you are ready, tell students exactly what you are doing and what to expect. Give them the justification and make them part of the "experiment."

To illustrate, here is what I say to students when I launch a new set of rules as an experiment or correct poor classroom management: "Students, we experience hurt feelings and disrupted learning because we are not all working with the same understanding. Together, we are going to make changes so everyone feels safe, loved, and valued. Most of all, we are going to protect our time so everyone has the best learning experience possible. Moving forward, we will practice two new rules, [X and Y]. We will practice these two rules and observe the outcomes for the next three weeks. Afterward, I want your feedback, and we will adjust accordingly. I care about each of you. Remember our goals for this year? Each of you will learn and have a positive experience! These new rules ensure we accomplish the goal for everyone."

Another way to gauge your classroom management is to find the master educators scattered throughout schools and districts. Observe teachers and look for examples/nonexamples of what a high-functioning classroom looks and feels like. Apply what you learn, and then ask a coworker or administrator to observe your classroom dynamic and provide honest feedback.

A fellow physics teacher once observed me and noticed I ask students on the left side of the classroom more questions than students sitting on the right side. I never knew this! Being right-handed, as I write on the board and pivot toward the students, I first see students to my left and immediately blurt out questions. I told students about the physic teacher's observations. They promptly informed me they were fully aware of the fact and gladly took right-side assigned seats because they were less likely to be called on. Without the insight of my coworker, students would still dread left-side seats. Observations are not for judgment but to help teachers perform better as educators. Lastly, reach out to the district. There is usually a gracious person who will gladly coach and mentor teachers through classroom management.

Safety Strategies

Even with flawless procedures and classroom management, every teacher can have one or more students with behavioral issues. One student's violent disruption holds a class hostage, robs learning time, and most importantly, compromises the safety of every individual present. Violence in any form, by any individual, is traumatic. Students and adults exposed to negative behavioral eruptions engage traumatic physiological responses. Such experiences are dangerous for all involved, including the difficult child, and can have lasting impact. The following process assists a teacher in systematically dealing with a difficult child to first, protect the entire class, and second, grow the child in need. The most practical, hands-on resource I read on this subject is *Behavior Code: A Practical Guide to Understanding the Most Challenging Students* by Jessica Minahan and Nancy Rappaport. When you recognize a challenging student in the classroom, read this book immediately – within 24 hours! The process outlined next basically summarizes the authors' insightful recommendations with a few additions (2012).

To begin, when a student has an outburst, respond intuitively and consistently. Make a mental note to watch if it happens again. According to Minahan, you need to classify the incidence as anxiety-related, oppositional, withdrawn, or sexualized behavior. If the behavior persists, tackle the process of protecting the class and growing the child with three steps: Observe, Accommodate, and Create (Minahan, 2012).

Observe

The observation step mimics detective work. Ultimately, a teacher identifies patterns in behavior and triggers. After each outburst, record everything that transpired before the burst and exactly what the child did and said. Minahan claims at least five observations are necessary to accurately identify what triggers the behavior and to classify the response.

Even though it seems counterintuitive during the observation period, in order to maintain the rest of the class, manage the difficult child by giving them what they want. This is a process that takes time. No quick fix, band aid, or superficial attempt to handle interruptions protect the students, including the challenging student. A minimum of five occurrences to collect data and clearly identify triggers and classify behavior will pay off down the road.

Crucial to this step is probing root cause. Minahan recognizes four possible causes for negative behavioral responses: escape, attention, sensory response, or tangible object (2012). Let's say a child cowered prior to math lessons to escape the fear and frustration of math work. After the five or more outbursts, a teacher can articulate triggers (transitions, content, activities, etc.), classify the behavior (anxiety-related, oppositional, withdrawn, or sexualized), and pinpoint root cause (escape, attention, sensory response, or tangible object). In the example of the child, the teacher identifies math content induces anxiety-related behavior as a means of escape.

Accommodate

Now the work begins in the form of modifications and accommodations. Enlist all adults interacting with the child. Design a plan for everyone to consistently apply. Teacher, counselors, specialists, administration, and parents together brainstorm healthy modifications to decrease frequency of behavioral disruptions and provide coping strategies for the child.

A variety of tools exist to accommodate students. Paramount among those is a relationship. The only way children grow is to trust adults who prioritize their best interest. An accepted, loved, cared for, valued child slowly responds with a malleable heart and open mindset. Invest extra time and attention to build a sincere, attentive relationship with the child. Share lunch together; discover favorite foods, activities, characters; know family member names; listen to stories; ask questions; smile often; let love shine through your eyes; and most importantly, genuinely care.

Consider this list of additional tactics: Establish predictable routines and make them visual and audible. Give warnings before breaks or transitions. Assign a lunch or recess buddy to remove the fear and shame of sitting or playing alone. Schedule additional breaks. Narrate thought processes to change perspective and provide positive self-talk. Allocate special jobs or leadership positions. When a student refuses to comply, simply state, "I understand." Then repeat your request. My vice principal reported that students usually comply after the third "I understand." One teacher told me she repeated the two words 10 times before the student positively responded. These are but a sampling of accommodation tools experts employ. Try different strategies to find the perfect modifications to help your students manage their own behavior.

Create

Thus far, the focus has centered on collecting data to understand then manage difficult student behavior. Once the behavior seems to be under better control, the best step in the process occurs. With the child's team, create a growth skill plan. Ultimately, the goal is for a child to leave a classroom a better, stronger, healthier person than they were when they first arrived. Considering a child's challenges, what tools can a team equip them with for success in life? Specifically look at social skills, self-regulation, and self-identification techniques. Model, practice, and prepare the child to recognize and control their thoughts and actions. Special education and child psychology experts provide the best resources to help develop a growth plan. Together as a team, create a skills outline in which everyone consistently participates and reinforces strategies.

The final component in protecting and fostering a safe school environment is a well-articulated school plan. Most schools probably have an intervention plan or written protocol for difficult child behavior responses. I also bet most teachers have no idea what the school plan actually says. It is one thing to have an official written statement and another to know and practice it.

With school leadership, find and scrutinize the current school plan in light of current student behavior and propose necessary amendments. Publicize the school plan for administration, faculty, parents, and students so all are informed. Then practice it consistently. A predictable school response to challenging behavioral and mental health outbursts supports effective classroom management.

Occasionally, I picture that sweet third-grade teacher sitting at the student table silently crying. Then I think of the boy and pray for God's healing to overcome the turmoil in his life. I end wondering about the 25 students who observed his violent actions day after day. Maybe children are changing, or maybe society is. Regardless, teachers must be equipped, supported, malleable, and adaptable when it comes to student behavior. Each person at school needs to feel safe and protected. Teachers are on the frontline in guaranteeing this fundamental right.

6S Summary

Teachers who naturally organize and keep things tidy typically love learning the Lean 6S process. Teachers who do not intuitively have organization skills also love learning about 6S. The former group embraces 6S as an affirmation of their practices and inner calm when things are clean. The latter group appreciates the straightforward, doable steps to become organized.

6S provides the perfect springboard into removing waste and sharpening practices with Lean Think tools. As a result, everything in a classroom or on a hard drive adds value. Each item sits in a purposefully assigned home and will abide in consistently tidy surroundings thanks to an organization system. All the pieces are now in place to move into the daily practice of incremental process improvement. Parameters rest in front of the teacher through the defined customer, goal, and measure. The current and ideal states show where a classroom is and where it is going. The foundation for success is well-established. Now the real work of Lean Think begins.

PART II: Waste

Chapter 7: Out With the Waste

Every November, the first week of second term, general and honors chemistry students begin Chapter 9: Chemical Reactions. Every year I also tell them about my wonderful Senior Pastor, Alex Lucero, a man who loves God, loves people, and also derives great joy from preaching, which means he usually goes over time on Sunday mornings. Predictably, a good 20 minutes into his sermon, he says, "And that is just my introduction." The congregation chuckles because there are only 15 minutes left of church. But no worries. Everyone listens and relishes the rest of the sermon, and then leaves 10 minutes later than intended.

In a similar scenario, my students, thus far in the school year, learned more new vocabulary than any language class, discovered atomic structure with calculations and placement on the periodic table, and correctly identified two different types of chemical bonds. First term is a shock to their teenage systems; they feel like salmon struggling to swim upstream. It is at this point I tell them that everything so far has been an introduction, a foundation, to learn and apply chemistry. So, with a huge smile on my face and slightly mischievous eyes, I proclaim, "Welcome to chemistry! Now the real work begins." The students groan, roll their eyes, and throw back their heads. I quickly step in to reassure them that laying a foundation requires accuracy and labor. Of course, first term is hard. However, because a solid chemical education now resides in their brains, the fun begins with hands-on chemistry. We kick it off with chemical reactions. They see two engaging demos and then personally perform two chemical reactions with gas evolving and combusting, forming new products, and changing colors. The groans morph into ooohs and aaaahs of delight.

We have arrived at a similar moment in this book. The ideology of Lean Think is meticulously outlined with kaizen, or incremental process improvement. The mobilization of energy to prepare and get ready for kaizen is described in the parameters and defining the customer, goal, and measure, and then identifying the current and ideal states. The last piece of the foundation is embodied in 6S and getting organized. Just like my students require fundamental skills to advance into chemical application, teachers undergo a paradigm shift with Lean Think to see education through a new lens. Everything up to this point has been an introduction, a foundation upon which a strong and successful classroom experience for both teacher and student is built. It is time to build and do some fun experiments. "Welcome to Lean Think! Now the real work begins."

What Is Waste?

Recall the concept of value from Chapter 3. Anything that moves the customer closer to the goal as reflected by the measure is value. Waste is everything that does not do that. Here is the No. 1 takeaway regarding waste: DO NOT KEEP IT! If something does not add value, then do not expend time, energy, or resources on it. It is a waste – in every possible way.

How often has a teacher sighed while listening in faculty meetings/professional development about the next initiative, the next set of rules, the next requirements, the next fabulous activities, the next new technology, etc.? They are expected to adopt the "next" big thing without removing anything from an already overflowing plate of responsibility and work. I remember thinking, "Please just let me go into my room, close my door, and do what I do best — teach children." Well, now teachers can, with justification, if they are focused on keeping only what truly adds value.

Before going any further, I must share a disclaimer. Some activities that do not increase student learning are still absolutely required. Lean Manufacturing calls it Necessary Non-Value Added Waste. Examples include taking roll, listening to announcements, administering school surveys, students moving from the classroom to the lab, or putting away workbooks. None of these tasks move learning forward but they are unavoidable. The trick is to decrease and minimize non-value-added waste as much as possible. A classroom's Future State ideally moves a student consistently through learning processes each second of a class. Clearly, even the best classroom will never achieve such condition 100% of the time. Non-value-added waste will always be present in some obligatory form, but teachers working with Lean Think principles continually work to decrease waste and increase value. So, boldly tackle waste removal by eradicating waste from practices; it opens space and time to focus on things that add value. The beauty in this process reveals itself in student performance: As waste decreases, value escalates, and students learn more. Fantastic!

There are nine wastes in education (Lean Education Enterprises, Inc., 2007). The next five chapters explain and provide examples for each waste. While reading about each waste, take the time to scan your classroom design, procedures, practices, expectations, and requirements. Mentally flag and compile a giant list of waste to throw out. Some waste can immediately be removed. Other waste takes energy and time to eliminate, but the investment pays off over time. The nine wastes include:

- Movement
- Time
- Overproduction
- Knowledge
- Talent
- Capacity

- Process and Handling
- Assets
- Defects

Where to Begin

At the outset, I share the premise of Lean Think and waste removal with students. I tell them I respect my time and their time. Everything I give or ask them to do is with strategic, thoughtful purpose to add value to their learning experience. That single statement forms strong bridges of trust and opens students' hearts to give me and my class a chance. I periodically verbalize and point out waste removal so students see the principle in action.

Make a firm commitment to that principle. Let it shape perspective and classroom approach and watch the benefits easily surface. First, waste is removed! No one wants to give away time or energy to unproductive efforts. The thought of wasting personal resources generates stress. All people want their actions and investments to have meaning and usefulness. Eliminating waste allows gifts and talents to grow lasting, quality fruit in life. Second, removing waste opens space and time for things that add value. A favorite of mine is seeing teachers work less outside of contract time. Educators better balance work and life by removing waste; a greater line of differentiation exists between the spheres. The absence of waste allows for time and space to improve upon the great things already happening in the classroom that increase value.

My husband often tells teachers at workshops — NOT ONE NEW THING! Focus on getting rid of stuff. Purge the waste. Drill the question, "Does this add value?" The first year my team and I implemented Lean Think, we only removed waste. Not until the second year did we apply tools to add more value. Especially focus on identifying value as defined by the goal and the measure. Everything else, throw it out. Not one new thing until the waste is removed.

There are four hacks to recognizing and removing waste:

- Identify root cause
- Grab the low hanging fruit
- Triage
- Solicit student feedback

Root Cause

Identifying root cause means probing an issue to ultimately fix the problem, not just treat a symptom. The root cause of most issues typically comes from one of two mindsets: don't know or don't care. The source of a problem stems from a lack of knowledge or understanding. Or, the problem originates because someone does not care about the issue enough to do the task correctly. Industry provides an excellent example of a 5 Whys probe. A manufacturer faithfully places warning labels on electrical appliances only to have them fall off before shipping. The labels have never fallen off before. Why are they falling off now? The project engineer just applied the first *why* question and continues until the root cause is discovered. The probe includes asking: Is it the adhesive, the paper, or the item's plastic coating that causes the label not to stick? The engineer learns that a subcontractor prints the labels, and the in-house team has not changed any variables. So, the engineer calls the subcontractor and, through another series of questions, finds out they used the wrong adhesive on those labels. Ah, the root cause is revealed and easily fixed with new labels made with the correct adhesive.

Several years ago, a darling, 15-year-old girl sat in my fifth period general chemistry class. She didn't turn in much homework but, much to my pleasure, liberally asked questions in class. In the middle of third term, her mother gave birth to twin baby boys which thrilled this young lady to the very core. Because she had excellent attendance, it was unusual for this student to be absent several weeks after the babies' birth. After the first week, I emailed the parent with my concern only to receive an email reply from my student about illness. After the second week, still no student. So, I started my 5 Whys investigation. Things did not make sense; I knew something was amiss and had to get to the root cause. Several email correspondences transpired but the stories were clouded and confusing, so I kept probing.

After three weeks, I still had no student! Desperate, I engaged the next level of intervention and recruited the help of a counselor. The counselor deftly connected with the parent via phone only to find out my student had been babysitting her baby brothers. The single mother needed to return to work but lacked child care. The counselor secured support and contacts for the parent, and the very next morning, my inquisitive student sat in the back row ready to fire chemistry questions at me again.

The exclusive solution to that problem, child care, was dependent on discovering the unique cause of the symptom, my student's excessive absences. When the root cause unfolded, the problem quickly became fixable and it dissolved. Numerous wastes plagued this situation, and dealing directly with the root cause removed each waste.

Low Hanging Fruit

In the fall, my sweet mother-in-law enjoys making plum jam from our two Damson Purple Plum trees. My husband dutifully unhooks the ladder hanging in the garage to place it against the plum trees. He climbs the tree to pick the high, sweet fruit while my mother-in-law stays on the ground and picks fruit within arm's reach, the low hanging fruit.

Likewise, a favorite tactic of teachers is to go for the low hanging fruit, so do the same thing with waste. Where are the quick wins, the fast, easy changes that immediately remove waste and increase value in the classroom? Just like standing in place and with one swipe of the hand, plums are in the basket; standing right where you are, what waste can you quickly eradicate from your teaching practices? My low hanging fruit examples include: removing AP chemistry term projects, dumping the even problems from student assignments, and not grading all sections of the lab rubric for every lab. I made each of these decisions after pressing myself to answer, "Does this add value for students to learn chemistry as reflected on the measure?" And to each question, I answered an emphatic NO. Each represented wasted talent, time, overproduction, movement, knowledge, and processing for both my students and me.

I enjoyed instant, positive results by removing the low hanging fruit of waste. For example, in lieu of AP students pouring energy into worthless term projects, students spent more time reviewing and preparing for exams. Instead of grading entire lab reports students did not review, I focused on one skill per lab and graded only that section of the rubric. I then held students accountable to fix and respond to the grading, something that is truly valuable. Find the quick wins and remove the accessible waste. All involved will enjoy more value.

Triage

Having five little girls in six years, I lived in a constant state of triage. On any given day, one child ate dirt in the corner of the yard, two fought over a scooter, another cried from a scraped knee, and the fifth ran after a ball rolling into the street. A mother's order for triage? Grab the child before she reaches the street, backtrack and tell the squabbling sisters to take turns, then pick up the crying child on the way to help the last daughter spit pica from her mouth. Same goes for teachers: Prioritize the triage based on urgency and impact.

As wastes surface, rate them according to which wastes rob the most value. Then, focus your energy and attention on first removing what hemorrhages value the most. For example, in my first-year teaching without Lean Think, it took six hours to grade free response tests for each unit. After performing all my low hanging waste removal during the next school year, grading tests proved the largest waste. It represented the triage priority because it offered little value (a single score) for significant hours of my time (during which no student learning occurred).

In year two with Lean Think, I invested one hour per test to create grading rubrics. Directly following a test, students exchanged exams, and each used a rubric to grade one another's work. The process saved me five hours of time per unit exam, students experienced examples/nonexamples by implementing the rubric, and they benefited from immediate feedback. The principle of triage applied to waste removal requires an upfront cost of energy and time. The backend savings of energy and time, however, are multiplied many times over the initial commitment.

Feedback

The line between waste and value can sometimes be blurred. In this case, do an experiment and let the students be part of it. Perform the activity or use the item, then collect data to see how students did. Test for student learning, the level they achieved, or the volume of learning they absorbed. Then ask the students for feedback. What did they think? How effective was the tool? Have the students rate the activity or item based on value added to learning and compare ratings with data. A clear picture typically emerges to categorize the entity as waste or value. As an example, I easily made 10,000 gradebook entries every term because of recording daily starters in addition to assignments, labs, and exams. It was unclear if grading starters added value to student learning. I told the students we were going to experiment through the year with different models of starter grading. First term, I recorded every starter grade. Second term, the students tallied starter scores at midterm and at the end of the term for a total of two starter gradebook entries per student in 10 weeks. Third term, I recorded one final tally of starter scores at the end of the term. Fourth term students still did starters but did not grade them, hence no scores were recorded. What were the results?

Amazingly, exam performance did not change across the nine school months, even with different models of grading frequency or not grading starters. I surveyed the students for feedback. The overwhelming consensus was that starters themselves were of great value but students found zero value in scoring them. Students said the starters reengaged prior learning and provided immediate feedback to resolve misconceptions. They felt accountable to do the starter with integrity because of my proximity, walking through the classroom during the first five minutes of class, and because I randomly cold called answers. The value was in doing the starter, not grading the starter. Now, the students do starters daily without grading or my recording scores. Student feedback proved highly beneficial in pinpointing the value or lack thereof in grading starters. Remember to solicit student feedback to determine waste and value when appropriate.

The bottom line is that removing waste from your classroom will be extremely satisfying. It accomplishes everything you want: no waste of your time and energy … or your students'!

Chapter 8: Heavy Hitters

Going back to the list of nine wastes, the first two, movement and time, are the biggest and easiest to remove. Jot down notes where these wastes can be immediately removed for quick wins, and then identify other wastes that may take time but offer significant rewards, thus adding more value in the classroom.

Movement

The waste of movement is any motion or transportation of a person, item, or document that does not add value to student learning. Note that movement includes physical and electronic objects. Break movement into three categories: motion of people, resources, and electronic entities.

To begin, think about the movement of students in your classroom. As students take steps to gather supplies, relocate to collaborative groups, or wander to visit with friends, do they learn? No. My most egregious example of movement waste was exposed my second year of teaching. I created an impressive supply station on a tiered shelf adjacent to the classroom door. It was the first thing students saw as they entered. Everything they needed sat neatly in multiples, organized perfectly. It made sense in my head to consolidate all supplies into one spot so everyone knew exactly where to access supplies and where to put them back. Plus, it looked pretty.

However, as you stand in the front center of the room, the supply station and door anchor the top right corner. The bottom left corner houses student folders. A diagonal line cuts the room in half from the supply station to the student baskets. When I set students free to turn work into their folders, I observed 40 students meandering to the supply station on the right side of the room. They stood in line, chatting away, and used the supplies to staple, cut, paste, etc. Then they ambled around the perimeter of the room to get to the opposite corner and endured another line, still talking, to turn in their assignment. How many wasted steps — and time!

Realizing this, I disassembled my glorious supply station in short order. I quickly pared down one giant supply depot to four miniature versions. One mini supply station remained in the original place of honor, another sat directly next to the student baskets in the front left corner, a new station secured the back left corner, and the last station sat in the back of the lab.

The supply solution places items where needed for easy access when needed. Most required supply usage derives from lab work, i.e., gluing in data or cutting out tables, etc. With a supply station in the lab, the students use tools when and where wanted — in and during the lab! For students who need supplies before they turn in work, the tools are readily available sitting adjacent to student baskets. As they turn in homework and need a stapler, they take no additional steps to grab the stapler because it is right there. I left supply stations in the back of the room for proximity to students sitting near those areas. Students already walking past a supply station simply stop to use tools without taking extra steps. Additionally, it decreases congestion at the other supply stations.

The goal is to devise ways for students to take as few steps as possible between rotations, accessing or returning resources, turning in work, or performing activities. By changing my supply station, I decreased average student steps by 25 steps for just one activity. It also decreased the amount of time to turn in work by over three minutes. Three minutes daily in a school year is 270 minutes, or 4.5 teaching hours. I just bought myself a half day in teaching time. Three extra minutes every day can mean more review, reteaching, questions, or summaries.

Now think about items moving. When I pass papers down a row, how many people touched the last paper in the row? In my case, 10. That is a waste of motion. Now, I place papers in a tray by the door. Students each take one paper as they come in. One person touches one paper; it moves exactly from point A to point B just as I intended, from me into the student's hands. Movement and time are no longer wasted passing out papers. Likewise, having multiples of popular items helps decrease the waste of motion. Rather than pass one stapler around the room for use, there are four staplers available in strategic locations. Watch items in a classroom zigzag from person to person, table to table, and devise solutions to decrease the movement of the objects.

Due to the boom of technology, electronic motion takes significant space in the lives of both teachers and students. Searching for electronic documents, looking for information, accessing programs, and navigating websites represent forms of electronic motion. Fewer clicks, faster access, and easier access to information all contribute to less waste in electronic motion. Ideally, teachers and students should know exactly how and where to connect with what they need with the fewest clicks possible.

I eradicated significant electronic motion waste the first year I used an e-book for honors chemistry. It took the students a solid five minutes to log into the e-book with typing, several clicks, and waiting to access homework. And this was after they already looked at my website for the actual assignment. At this point, homework only showed the problems. No adaptive or interactive capabilities existed. All 150 students each waited five minutes, three times a week to log onto the e-book just to see a picture of the homework problems. The cumulative cost of time and motion for my honors students racked up to 22.5 hours a week — for no gains in learning.

To remove the waste, I took screenshots of the e-book homework and uploaded them as PDF files on my school website. The students decreased their motion from a lengthy logon process to one click on my website which they visited each time anyway. Not only did motion decrease, but the time on this task also decreased from five minutes to only seconds. It took me 10 minutes a week to upload the files, but it was well worth my small investment of time to save students a collective 22 hours a week of waste. So, begin thinking in terms of collective and individual motion and time. Measure steps and clock movement. You will be amazed at the waste discovered through motion of people, items, and electronics.

There's a caveat in the waste of motion. Movement for children is valuable when used purposefully. Children need to move; in fact, movement can be a form of learning, and therein lies the key. Intentionally plan movement for children. For instance, when instruction hits saturation for young minds, they need a brain dump. (For moving working memory to short-term memory, see Chapter 14.) At that strategic moment, the teacher then guides children to relocate to reading groups, which tactically controls movement opportunities to add value in the learning experience.

The important thing is to become aware of your movement, your students' movement, and the movement of resources. The goal is minimal movement to focus student learning. Topping off the newfound discovery of movement and waste, here is a rapid-fire list of scenarios you can look at.

- Searching for:
    - Supplies
    - Documents, physical or electronic
    - Location
    - Resources
- Transitions:
    - Make it a game or competition
    - Count steps or time transitions

- Looking for information:
  - o Do they ask: "Teacher, where are the instructions?"
  - o Teachers lacking information from students, parents, or administration
- Physical movement (applies to teachers and students):
  - o To access resources
  - o To relocate
  - o Placement of objects and how it impacts movement (6S Straighten step)

Time

The excess, idle, or unwise use of time is wasted time. Misappropriation of time is one of the largest waste culprits in classrooms. Recall the ideal state, where our customer learns every moment. Students sit in my class for 90 minutes per period. A zero waste of time would mean my students are moving through the learning process, engaging active thought, and discovering new concepts every second of the 90 minutes. But is this realistic? Do not become overwhelmed. Remember, Lean Think is *incremental* process improvement. One step at a time, teachers remove waste and get closer to the ideal state. Honestly, I still have minutes tick away in my class period with no learning. I continually observe and then experiment how to remove the waste of time so more moments embody productive learning.

Not surprisingly, the majority of time wasted is due to WAITING. Whenever a student or teacher waits, priceless minutes evaporate, unused. At the root, a child's waiting mind is idle, no learning transpires, and precious educational seconds are gone forever. Students experience idle, wasted time while standing in line, sitting in desks waiting to learn, waiting for instructions, getting/returning items, or passing out papers. Students' brains wait to be engaged, challenged, pushed, and stretched.

I discovered my most profound blunder wasting students' time after I videoed classes turning in papers five minutes before the end of class. It was truly shocking. (Sidenote: You see things differently through video. Watching actions on a screen rather than in person gives new perspective.) At the end of class, my mind and hands were scurrying, I assumed students, too, must be busy tying off the learning day, right? The video proved otherwise.

I had not recognized the full impact of 40 students standing in line to turn in papers. One basket sat in the front left corner of the class with hanging files for each student. The young people dutifully lined up to wait, and one by one, they orderly placed homework in their manilla folders. Many students talked while others stood bored out of their minds, casting glazed, blank stares. It was depressing to watch. My system created a bottleneck, thus wasting the last five minutes of student time. Every teacher knows five minutes at the end of class is golden. It is the grand finale to repeat objectives, answer final questions, review main takeaways, have student partner share, write summaries, or reiterate content. I forfeited powerful learning time to worthlessly standing in line.

My immediate solution disbanded the bottleneck that created the terrible line. I moved the last half of the student alphabet to a second basket and placed it in the opposite, back left corner of the room. Only half the students would now be in each area. Also, rather than put the baskets against walls, I pulled them to the end of the tables so students could surround them on three sides. The next day in class, I told the students I appreciated their polite, systematic behavior; however, turning in papers was no longer the place to practice such restraint. I gave instructions, and permission, to turn in papers as quickly as possible with multiple people accessing the baskets. Three students at a time (one in front and one on each side of the basket) placed papers in their folders. Instead of one student turning in a paper at any moment, six students turned in papers (three at each basket).

Then it became a game. I timed each class and recorded minutes on the board. What originally took each class nearly five minutes to accomplish, dwindled to a mere 45 seconds. The inane act of turning in homework no longer took up four minutes of valuable learning time. Within a school year, each class period added six hours of learning time back to the value pile (four minutes multiplied by 90 days). Minutes make a difference; even seconds make a difference.

Teachers also battle waste in the form of their own waiting, as every educator can attest: waiting for permission, information, or directions. They wait for supplies, projects, and edits. When teacher time is wasted, student time is wasted, and both are equally detrimental.

Another potential waste of time involves not enough quiet time. Avoid the pitfall of automatically mistaking quiet time as idle time. The two are not synonymous. Teachers remove and evade idle waiting like the plague. Quiet time, however, provides a potent learning tool. Students and teachers *need* time to process, formulate, create, dream, and synthesize. Just because I consume my students' time with productive, learning activity does not ensure I used it for optimum value. Without providing time to discuss, write, ponder, reflect, and think, students are robbed of the opportunity to make final connections and grow. The same is true for teachers. Educators require time to process ideas and plans, sometimes grumbling, "I just need five seconds so I can completely put two thoughts together!"

A balance exists in how we use time for overt learning actions and thoughtful mental reflection. Avoiding wasted time in Lean Think does not mean students (or teachers) are robots who continuously work, work, work. Teachers understand this. Students need mental breaks so they can continue learning at optimum levels. The key lies in differentiating allotments of time for both fruitful activity and quiet consideration. They equally add value in the correct proportions, which varies from class to class, content to content. The best person to decide how much time to allocate to each means of learning is the expert in the classroom, the teacher.

This leads to the last aspect of time: enough. Teachers strive to find the "time sweet spot" for every activity, which means to give students just enough time to add the utmost value and then move on to dodge waste. Experience and experimentation are the answers. New teachers especially face the challenge of effectively pacing activities and overall class time management because of their lack of experience. Even seasoned teachers periodically question appropriate amounts of time for various activities.

However, just being thoughtful and purposeful about time management helps remove waste and increase productivity. Experiment with time allocation and write down data. Timing my students turning in homework revealed useful information to both students and me. The stopwatch, however, does not answer every timing question. Many teachers confess they need more time for review or reteaching but cannot eke out space to fit it in. To tackle this problem, experiment with the goal in mind. Remember your goal and measure and keep going back to it while designing new tactics. Time is finite; it may come down to what adds the *most* value or thinking outside of the box about learning alternatives. The goal and measure are the barometer to determine what adds the most value or ignites creativity to approach a problem from a different angle. Look at two examples from my classroom.

For years, my AP students complained they saw no connection between classroom content and lab practices. The labs confused young scholars and seemed like a waste of time even though I knew the practices reflected lessons taught in lecture. I had a hunch the disconnect resulted from a lack of post-lab discussion. Lab days easily ran from bell to bell, and even then, students rushed just to finish long lists of laboratory procedures. I brought the issue to my husband. He always shares great ideas.

My husband asked me to write down exactly everything students did for 90 minutes on lab days: starter, agenda, review homework questions, pre-lab discussion, go to lab, and perform the lab. Looking at my list, he posed a question that may seem obvious to others but never crossed my mind. "Do you have to do the starter, agenda, and homework review on lab days?" My initial thought was, of course! We do those items every day; it is part of our routine! He then pressed me on value and goals: State the goal for the class, identify the goal for lab days, and list the most valuable activities on lab day. Then it hit me. The beginning activities (starter, agenda, and homework review) added significant value to the overall class but not to lab days. The greatest value of lab days came from doing and discussing the lab.

My husband suggested the students begin in the lab, skip the classroom with the beginning activities entirely, and use the extra time at the end of the class period for class discussion. Brilliant idea, but one last obstacle stood in the way. I needed a whiteboard to lead the post-lab discussion and the lab space did not have one. He then said he would hang one himself. So, he did.

Back at school, I prepped the students with the procedural change and gave the reasoning behind the shift. The responsibility to look at the agenda online was on them. All homework questions would have to be addressed individually before or after school. With the starter removed, everyone was expected to be at their lab station, ready to work, by the time the tardy bell rang.

The first lab proceeded without incident. Best of all, every student completed the lab with 15 minutes to spare which opened thoughtful discussion of data, application, errors, and conclusions. This tied book learning to hands-on experiences. As a teacher, it was one of those rare moments when you feel warm inside because something worked the way you wanted it to the first time.

Now, my AP labs consistently follow this pattern to leave time for post-lab discussion. It turns out the beginning activities add value, but post-lab discussion adds *more* value. I had to experiment, identifying what added the most value in a given amount of time. Insisting students perform routine, opening activities, although valuable in most scenarios, wasted valuable lab time. To invest student time with optimum returns, frame your goal, list your activities, and then apply the filter, "Does this add value?" You may even need to ask, "What adds the most value?" In addition to determining what adds the most value based on the goal when evaluating multiple valuable items, I push the status quo. The comfort of the familiar, "This is how it has always been done", must be set aside. I never imagined a class period skipping opening class procedures and immediately beginning in the lab. A focus on both the overarching and task goals lead the way for me to try something different and maximize time.

Another situation prompted a creative response to protect and fully utilize time, COVID-19. My school schedule changed five times within one year after the outbreak of the pandemic. How to protect and take full advantage of each in-person second became my passionate focus. I executed dozens of experiments, and failed often, but I walked away with two wins. First, because I did not see students consistently or at the same time, I let go of turning in daily assignments and created "playlists." (See Chapter 17.) To begin, each student was given the same list of homework to complete weekly by Sunday at midnight. Provided with several resources and avenues for learning, the students chose when to complete homework within a seven-day period. Eventually, I modified the lists for exceptionally high and low learners. The students responded positively. The flexibility accommodated the varied situations they all faced. It gave enough of a framework to hold students accountable, assist in organizing time, keep students current in learning, yet provide customization to remove undue time pressure. Student feedback showed they loved the design of what I now call "teacher guided, student self-regulation." I kept the playlists past COVID-19, something I would not have predicted. The playlists remove the waste of time on several levels and add value. Win-win!

Second, I moved fully to digital homework for all my chemistry classes. Bear in mind, I clinched my teeth and resisted online homework for several years. Like so many, change hit my classroom like a speeding freight train thanks to quarantines. It just so happened that I had purchased new AP books, with online companions, the year prior to the pandemic. Then, when it struck,

I picked up a new prep as an adjunct professor for a state university, and the class came with an online book. I had resources before I knew I needed them.

The adaptive learning components, online resources, and most of all, scaffolded question tutorials filled in the gaps for so much missed in-person instruction. My epiphany observing this process was that learning time is not restricted to my physical classroom. Granted, the most effective learning happens one on one, but teaching moments can also occur outside the walls of Room 2314.

Rather than begrudging or mourning this fact, I choose to embrace the wonderful idea that I am given more than 90 minutes every other day. When this paradigm shift finally took hold in my brain, I wanted to exploit every possible minute the students touched chemistry *outside* of my class. The e-books do just that. They teach in my absence! Talk about maximizing time.

To summarize, remember that several facets embody the waste of time. The quickest win removes waiting in the classroom. Anytime a student or teacher wait for something, time is wasted. Balance this concept with the understanding that quiet time is not the same as idle time. And lastly, honestly question the value of how time is utilized in the classroom. Is just the right amount of time appropriately allocated to each task to maximize value? Teachers also need time to process and formulate information. Not being given enough of time to do that constitutes waste, too. And when a teacher's time is wasted, student time is also wasted in the long run. Here is a rapid-fire list of examples where time is most wasted.

- Students
    o Turning in work
    o Retrieving/returning supplies
    o Interruptions
    o Passing out papers
    o Standing in line
    o Waiting for information
    o Waiting for answers to questions

- o Not enough time to process, create, dream, review, question
- Teachers:
  - o Waiting for permission
  - o Waiting for information
  - o Waiting for supplies/equipment
  - o Waiting for direction

Chapter 9: Don't Give Away the Farm

The next four of the nine wastes reveal how teachers and students overuse, underuse or do not use the value they already have. Optimizing value deploys strengths and resources in the right amount at the right time. The wastes include overproduction, knowledge, talent, and capacity. This chapter explores the waste of overproduction.

Overproduction

Many teachers fall prey to overproduction waste, the misguided notion that the more time something takes, the more energy expended, the harder the task … the more valuable it is. Most teachers want to do a fantastic job, sacrificing themselves as evidence, thinking extra effort must translate into improved student learning. On the contrary, more does not always mean better.

Overproduction is doing more than is needed to realize true gains, or to add true value. It breaks down into two simple categories: giving too much of oneself or requiring too much of students. The Lean Think mindset establishes that every second a student is in class, learning happens. Guarding precious educational moments necessitates the perfect amount of information and effort throughout the learning process. This sweet spot, the balance between doing and moving on, goes back to asking, "Does this add value to accomplish the goal as reflected in the measure?"

Erasing overproduction identifies the areas where minimum effort yields maximum value. Just because I am working hard does not mean it accomplishes the goal. Teachers and students can give 110%, but removing the overproduction in that effort ensures all 110% produces value. It's true: Educators often experience guilt letting go overproduction because they feel like they are not doing enough. An engrained academic ideology pushes teachers to go the extra mile, and if they do not, then they have compromised student learning somehow. What if the extra mile does not add value to student learning? What if, instead, isolating and eradicating unfruitful energy, time, and effort liberates and frees teachers to add more value with the same high achieving standards? Then student learning truly grows. As teachers focus on only doing and requiring what adds value, overproduction vanishes and additional time, space, and resources open to add even more value.

I fell prey to overproduction under the guise of "working hard" many times. The previous example of grading all starters, 10,000 entries per term, illustrates my sincere effort to do well yet miss the mark. Sadly, all the energy spent recording and entering starters produced no value in student learning, as I later learned. Not only have I given too much, done too much, or worked too hard — only to have labor evaporate — but I have also required too much of the students. In my first years teaching, I assigned the students far too many homework problems. Part of the problem was that I love chemistry, as in *geeky* love chemistry. If students can do five problems, why not 10? Because who am I kidding? Doing chemistry homework is like eating candy. Right? Maybe for me, but I discovered students lack a sweet tooth for chemistry coursework. Busy work also fits in this category. Just because students are occupied doing work does not mean value is added to their learning experience.

Now, I purposefully choose every problem students do to accomplish a goal to move learning forward. When students learn, then master, a concept, I do not require any more work. Of course, as good practice, I circle back to the content with review problems, ensuring retention. However, if students only need seven problems to show proficiency, acquire needed skills, and effectively practice, then they only do seven problems. I no longer give 12 problems "for fun."

Today, I constantly reevaluate the perfect amount of homework. It differs for different students, but the majority fall into a bell curve of the right amount of homework to add maximum value with minimum effort. I openly let the students in on this principle. Each problem highlighted in yellow on my course page signifies the ideal amount of homework to master chemistry in my class, no more and no less. I never assign an extra problem that does not add value to student learning, and the students know it.

About Grading

Repeatedly, teachers express frustration with grading. Grading is an overproduction magnet. Think about this first idea. I love my red pen and giving feedback. If I spend hours grading papers with my beloved crimson writing utensil and students do not read or respond to remarks, did my efforts add value to student learning? No. The quandary manifests in the fact that the feedback itself is very valuable, but if students do not digest the feedback, it does not help them.

Now consider this second idea. Does grading every component of every task every time add value? Of course not. If nothing else, too much feedback overwhelms the students and prevents adequate processing. More importantly, is every facet of understanding really being assessed? Most likely only one or two skills, a cluster of content, or single application is the intended focus. Grade what is taught now, not everything taught the last four months or prior knowledge from the past two years. Specifically assess skills and knowledge related to a teaching cycle. My husband and I like to quote from *Star Wars: A New Hope*: "Stay on target!" What do students need to learn and be able to do from this unit? Grade that only, and both teacher and students will be on target.

Focus grading on the focus of learning. The operative word is "focus." Pinpoint what truly needs to be assessed through any given activity, project, exam, assignment, etc. If the learning focus is how to write a topic sentence, then grade topic sentences. Do not grade punctuation or essay structure. Notice what I am doing: I am officially giving permission not to grade everything on every submitted piece of work. By emphasizing a learning topic and specifically grading just that topic, it focuses students' minds and produces better results. Less distracted and scattered by feedback overload, students more effectively process the actual goal of the lesson because of the focused learning and grading.

Concentrating on the goal, measure, and value fundamentally breaks the shackles of over-grading. Genuinely reflect on how grading increases student learning and how grading adds value to accomplish the goal as reflected in the measure. Remove activities that lack power to propel academic growth.

I learned this lesson after laboring, after contract time, over AP Free Response Questions (FRQs) for each chapter. As mentioned earlier, I graded every AP Test FRQ. Insightful red marks filled students' exams, taking hours of my time but returning no student benefits. Upon implementing rubrics and peer grading, students engaged the grading process and gleaned awareness from feedback. Additionally, accountability and higher-level thought emerged by requiring test corrections for each missed point. All this happened during class and did not require a minute of my personal time. Grading and the implications of the grade were much more meaningful to the students without my energies. More value was added to students, ironically, through my taking less time.

This example may not fit every classroom; however, as the expert in a setting, teachers find similar overproduction that, once removed and amended, will generate significant value for students with a fraction of educator effort. Be open and honest, weighing what you give compared to the value it offers. Then be willing to change. The huge gains made through this process profits both teachers and students.

Another option is to grade a section(s) rather than the entirety of an assignment. This is best illustrated by my honors chemistry lab notebooks. Every other week, students perform a lab and complete an entire lab write-up with title, date, objective, material, procedure, observations, data, results, calculations, conclusion, and evaluation. Multiply that by 150 students. I used to grade these bimonthly. Now I only grade every section for an entire lab once a term. The other labs have a grading focus, but they vary. For example, the first lab is graded completely on participation for sections present. Did the student include every section? It's easy points, yet it's surprising how many students forget the date or do not write an evaluation. The second lab of the year gets the "conclusion" emphasis in grading. I teach the students how to write a paragraph conclusion, including data discussion to justify learning statements. They hear and read examples. When grading, I quickly award participation points for simply having the other sections, but I read through the conclusions with a fine-toothed comb leaving remarks, as necessary.

I proceed through the first semester in this manner, focusing on one section of the rubric at a time. Each time, I make sure the students are fully aware of the critical area to be graded. By second semester, I tell students to prepare for surprises. I randomly choose one section for attentive grading, undisclosed to students. This saves me time grading while requiring students to do their best on each section. Again, the point is to focus the grading. It may require a section-by-section approach, a technique that proves effective in adding value to student learning while staving off overproduction.

Search for minimum effort for maximum value so efforts go to other valuable endeavors. It is worth sharing a tremendous grading hack from my school's English department. These teachers are exceptional. They also love Lean Think. They are fabulous instructors, passionate about content, and experts in classroom procedures, which includes grading. As many teachers can, they accurately predict the most common errors students make. Preemptively, they created a color code system. With different highlighters at the ready, they read essays. A yellow mark indicates issues with the thesis statement, pink denotes syntax errors, green communicates inference misinterpretation, etc. Students possess the corresponding key to what the colors mean, and respond with corrections accordingly. The teachers no longer write the same comments over and over. One swipe of a color tells students all they need to know to improve and move forward. Perform this same concept with numbers or letters instead of colors if preferred.

Another difficult grading topic comes from the arts: subjective grading. Right away people say to use a rubric. Emphatic yes, but easier said than done! Inherent in the word "subjective" is critique based on feelings and opinion. That leaves a very broad range for teachers to grade and students to aim for. Teachers become ensnared in overproduction by spending too much time grading, and some students inadvertently overproduce by investing more time and energy than is required or needed to add value.

Some tips and tricks help narrow subjective grading. The keys are to 1) divide the rubric into a) specific skills and b) creative input, and 2) clearly inform and model for students how to complete the rubric. Truthfully, the arts contain concrete, tangible, and measurable skills. For instance, a dance teacher wants dancers to name and demonstrate the five basic ballet positions. A band teacher evaluates how a student holds and cares for an instrument. An art teacher watches how a student holds and orients a brush in oil painting. Clearly outline in a rubric the specific knowledge and skills students must master.

Recently, while coaching junior high elective teachers, I heard statements like: I want students to put in effort, I want students to show passion, I want students to be interested, or I want students to care. A challenge of elective classes comes down to one fallacy: "This class is an easy A." How does a teacher inspire enthusiasm when students think all they need to do is show up to get an A? The creative rubric helps solve the problem. Clearly and articulately list what students must do to earn full points on each rubric section. List words like care, effort, passion, and interest. Then qualify the words with definitions. In class, provide examples, model desired behaviors, and highlight students exhibiting rubric traits. It is appropriate to grade and expect these qualities. Students just need to understand how to fulfill the creative characteristics and requirements.

One art teacher told me a student questioned their 6/10 grade while a neighboring student earned 10/10. The teacher explained that the 6/10 student's artwork was better than his neighbors, but he put in little effort, scoffing at the assignment with indifference. The student who earned the perfect score of 10/10 genuinely labored over the work but lacked the same talent. Grading by subjective standards is expected, but metrics need to be published, repeated, and clarified to justify scores when questioned. Also, put the rubric in student's hands before projects or performance preparations even begin. Clearly establish how to earn proficient points. Remind students of expectations and highlight excellent student examples often. If students must show passion as part of the grade, great! Show them how to show passion! These qualitative aspects of grading require ample illustration and reiteration.

Also, be prepared to explain and defend creative rubric grading to parents. The advantages include a concise checklist, especially for the left brained students who more comfortably manipulate computer code than a C major scale. They hold a doable, fair set of expectations that can be mastered without judgment of ability, or lack thereof. It removes some of the pressure teachers feel and labor over in grading creativity. Teachers know what they want to see, both in the creative process and final product. Students just need to know what that is and how to achieve it. Print and distribute the rubric, then reinforce it in front of the students.

Grading can be the bane of a classroom. Honestly evaluate the energy invested in grading versus resultant student growth. Solely grade what is taught to remove overproduction and focus students on the critical learning topic. Consider chunking the grading process into sections. Run with the ideas of color, number, or letter coding rubrics, and optimize the powerful tool of feedback.

Overworked

It happens: Some teachers genuinely have more tasks than time in the day and are genuinely overworked. In many cases, however, it is not a result of their teaching assignment; instead, they need to learn how to manage the profession efficiently. This was my situation and why I began Lean Think! The perspective change with value and waste consolidates our efforts to increase student learning in a reasonable amount of work time.

For a select few their teaching assignment physically mandates more time than the contract allots. Their schedule may contain six different contents, they teach different grade levels or content frequently, the content itself changes often (technology), or extra teaching activities rob prep time. Teachers with this kind of schedule experience overproduction due to an excessive workload. They require intervention and support outside of their classrooms. Administration and district leaders need to help.

The first approach looks at money. Talk to the head principal. Is there a way to apportion extra duty pay? Next, seek to get a teacher's aide or grading aide. Both could help bear the excess burden. Then pursue collaboration. Teachers in this scenario typically classify as "Singleton PLCs," the "one of" in a school. No one else in the school teaches what they teach, so they design, prepare, and evaluate alone. Contact similar content teachers in the district to produce resources together and share the weight. Then, look to the district. Ask the district to design a class equipped with everything needed as a "plug and play" model for singleton PLC teachers. Districts have great opportunity in this area. The perspective derives from simple math. For example, imagine a technology class where content changes every three years. Amendments to the class take 40 hours of preparation. Ten instructors teach this class in ten different schools. If all 10 teachers individually redesign the class (which often happens), they collectively invest 400 hours. Ten weeks of educational resources are consumed without one moment of direct student interaction. Additionally, those teachers typically absorb the extra work hours in personal time because "it comes with the job." This is overproduction waste. In Lean Think ideology, the overproduction waste implies disrespect and lack of human kindness toward workers. I understand this has been the modus operandi in education, but it can change.

In contrast, if one district specialist revamps the class and passes it to educators, only 40 hours are pulled from overall resources. The district employee gets paid without usurping personal time. In another approach, the district hires and pays a teacher, or a group of teachers, to work over the summer to produce the new curriculum and resources. Individual teachers then take the prepackaged course and tweak it to fit their personality and specific demographic. Ten teachers no longer reinvent the wheel; the district responsibly creates the wheel for all to benefit. Overproduction waste dissolves and professional respect reigns.

Overproduction robs teachers of well-intentioned resources. Whether a teacher gives more time and energy than adds value or a student fulfills requirements lacking in value, overproduction saps vital educational assets. Reclaimed precious resources now stand available to be spent in genuinely valuable pursuits. Here is a list of rapid-fire examples of overproduction in the classroom.

- Giving more information to students, parents, faculty, or administration than adds value
- Giving students more directions than the next step requires

- Teaching curriculum that is not assessed
- Collecting data or creating reports no one uses
- Requiring projects that do not add value
- Designing projects that are too long.
- Making too many copies or creating too many redundancies.
- Change for the sake of change
- Elaborate bulletin boards, classroom decorations, or extreme student-created parent gifts
- Extravagant art projects
- Duplicating work between colleagues
- Overusing someone's expertise or skill

Chapter 10: Information Everywhere

Every April for the first five years of teaching, I held AP chemistry reviews Tuesday and Thursday nights from 7:00-8:30 p.m. The students asked specific questions, and we practiced former Free Response Questions together. One day, while turning in my timecard, I overheard an AP Calculus teacher ask the head secretary which account to reference for AP extra duty pay. Intrigued, I pulled the teacher aside and inquired about the additional money. Come to find out, the school set aside AP funds yearly to compensate all AP teachers for reviews conducted outside of contract time. No one told me. I had hosted reviews to help students earn one more point on their final score, not for the money. But the money would have been nice! I had earned hundreds of dollars every year yet did not collect because of my lack of knowledge. Vital information was unknown to me.

Knowledge Wasted

A waste of knowledge is a lost opportunity to learn or recreate existing knowledge. My situation with the AP reviews reflects the first scenario. Information is out there for a teacher or student but remains inaccessible or unused. The second way to waste knowledge is to repeat information, an understanding, data, or skill already available or learned. Although mastery has been achieved or prior knowledge is solid, when a teacher or student must endure hearing it yet again, it's wasted time, too!

I Don't Know What I Don't Know

The question often arises: Is information published, accessible, or shared? Imagine a teacher needing or creating a student resource while, unknowingly, a peer has already made that very item. Unless that teacher shared the information or resource (knowledge), it is of no benefit collectively. Collaboration, transparency, and open sharing prevent this type of waste.

Several best practices foster an environment that make it more likely for knowledge to flow between colleagues and students. First, respect and psychological safety must be paramount. All people, educators and students, thrive in warm and accepting surroundings. Knowledge freely passes between people when the following mindset permeates a school:

- Ideas are accepted and stimulated.
- Creativity is valued.
- Suggestions are sincerely considered and enacted.
- Mistakes are used as stepping stones.
- Experimentation is encouraged.
- Open discussion thrives.
- Incremental, process improvement is the standard, not the exception.
- The individual is held in high esteem.

In a practical sense, the exchange of knowledge most easily occurs when useful channels are in place. Picture a suggestion box in the faculty room or a classroom. Teachers and administrators read and consider suggestions. Some are implemented, praised, or rewarded. The dynamic of a school or classroom changes from "us against them" to "we are in this together" when new knowledge and ideas are encouraged.

Consider a PLC meeting where the agenda consistently includes a one-minute reflection from each participant to share knowledge gained from an activity. For example, teachers share what they learned, what did not work, what worked well, and what students

liked or did not like about an activity. Regularly create
opportunities for individuals to communicate invaluable
knowledge and experience.

Lastly, practices and processes need to be published and
transparent. Ideally, the school office consolidates practical
processes into a reference document. Things like how to submit a
timecard, request leave, complete a purchase order request, or
conduct a fundraiser are concisely explained and housed in one
document. Include support processes such as extra duty pay,
behavior intervention, new class creation, or handling disgruntled
parents. Many terrific processes already exist in school offices,
administrative rolls, and counseling departments, they simply need
to be printed and distributed to most efficiently transfer knowledge
to faculty, parents, and students.

Data

A significant waste of knowledge in education is data. Data is the
product of measurements which confirm whether or not a goal is
achieved. Prolific data rests dormant or underutilized, yet it
represents potentially meaningful knowledge for teachers and
students. However, effectiveness of data depends on collection,
interpretation, and application. For example, sharing data between
PLC's fosters ingenuity and pinpoints successful tools. Passing
data in vertical alignment between grades or content areas prepares
teachers for new students and offers reflection on past student
performance. Tracking data year to year refines practices and
identifies independent variable effectiveness. Additionally, make
data transparent. Data regarding everything from formative
assessments to standardized national exams should be shared and
discussed. In a blame-free atmosphere, honestly identify successful
and unsuccessful practices. Only by exchanging data can growth
happen. A larger picture emerges as groups of educators look at
bigger sample sets with different variables. Evaluating data
together, with varied expertise and viewpoints, illuminates places
for improvement, confirms effective systems, and generates new
ideas.

Collecting data does not need to be overwhelming or time consuming, nor should data-sharing invoke fear, competition, or self-consciousness. The data is already there. Simply recording exam or project averages begins to paint a picture of student performance. For instance, in a single classroom, compare exam averages from unit to unit and evaluate tools implemented in comparison to results. What waste becomes apparent? Which tools shine? Which practices prove effective or ineffective?

Share data with colleagues in PLC or departments. This is not to show off or be shamed. As my PLC first began sharing data, the mindset shifted from "These are my students in my classroom," to "These are our students in our content." We are on the same team and work together for every student to succeed. Blame-free, honest, and safe discussions produce a better product for each teacher and student because it prevents knowledge waste. Then ask: "What adjustments can be made to improve as a team?" Exchanging knowledge through data and best practices bolsters everyone's classroom. Additionally, teachers share the workload by working together. Rather than writing every test, the work is divvyed up, and each teacher writes every third test. Disclosing data removes piles of waste, which greatly benefits teachers. Students, however, ultimately gain the most through teachers working together and sharing knowledge.

The last, what I call "golden nugget" of data collection and evaluation came from a master AP Calculus teacher. It is part of Lean Think but another teacher had to help me see it. After my difficult failure, first iteration, teaching AP chemistry, I sought seasoned advice from a legend. I asked this teacher if he would mind sharing his knowledge to help me become a better AP chemistry teacher. In his kind, gentle manner, he sat in one of my student desks eating a Cup of Noodles as I posed questions over lunch. Among the many wonderful ideas shared, he told me to begin collecting data from year to year. He insisted that the more accurate data picture I painted for students, the more driven and motivated they would be in class and in doing homework.

On his advice, I began a five-year journey. With the help of student para-instructors and a spreadsheet, I recorded every AP student's exam scores for the year. In July, when AP results posted, I dragged each student's data to the Excel section, matching the score they earned on the national exam. All students scoring a 5 collated in the same group and individual exam averages were calculated per section. This provided a goldmine of data. I can tell students on every test where they are trending with respect to the actual exam. For example, students who earned a 5 on the official exam averaged 81% on Exam 3. The knowledge provides a powerful and inspiring barometer for students from year to year, test by test.

This extensive data collection was not only hugely insightful in directing my instruction, but it also increased student engagement and bumped effort levels. I understand my classes are college level and it's easier to glean solid data. However, the principle applies to all levels of education. For instance, a kindergarten teacher may tell their darling, chubby-cheeked students that past pupils who mastered letter recognition and sounds by October read Level B books by the end of the school year. A music teacher may share that the No. 1 commonality between first chair instruments is each student securing that position mastered the Circle of Fifths major scales. Data inspires and challenges students to reach higher and work harder.

The data is there. It takes an observant eye, awareness of its value, and a passion to share that knowledge. Pick one project with easily accessible data. It can be as simple as recording exam averages. Most grading systems provide analytics that give much more than performance means, but start basic. The point is to establish the measure, collect data from the measure, and then *use* it. Teachers eliminate the waste of knowledge when they share and use data. Be the person who looks for data, asks for data, and shares data with both colleagues and students.

Again?

The second major waste of knowledge occurs when knowledge is repeated or duplicated. This is different from content review. Circling back for academic review solidifies understanding and confirms retention. A waste of knowledge occurs when teachers use precious resources to reteach something already mastered. Everyone recalls sitting in a class or meeting, inwardly groaning because they already know the information being presented. Frustrated, everyone complains inwardly: Do not waste my time! Teach me something new!

For teachers, the waste of knowledge creeps in through required meetings, trainings, or testing. Courteous reminders and reteaching are best distributed via email. Place as much into email communication as possible. However, the effectiveness of emails depends on them being read. Whenever possible, leave meeting time for new information, instruction, and discussion. A recommendation for academic leadership to consider: Tell your team that meeting time will be minimized and reserved for valuable new information and discussion, but only if everyone reads emails. Distributing information in emails will be the standard, but they must be read for meetings to be infrequent and brief.

As for mandatory trainings and tests, offer a "test out" option. For example, every year I am required to watch the same state child abuse PowerPoint. I can tell you what the next slide will say and list the interactive questions before they appear. Rather than have every teacher across the state sit for 45 minutes each August to watch the same PowerPoint, offer a final test. Teachers will take the test with one of two outcomes: Teachers pass the exam, hence demonstrating proficiency in the material, download a certificate with a mere 10-minute investment and walk away. Or teachers who do not pass the test will watch the PowerPoint, pushing through interactive questions to gain valuable understanding. How many thousands of teacher hours across the state would be saved and then reserved to add value to students through a proficiency test?

This is also true for trainings. Offer a test-out option to demonstrate understanding or a skill. If someone is competent in an area, allow them to show it. When competency is confirmed, award it. A false idea exists, mostly from habit, that seat time equates to learning. If a person already possesses knowledge or skill, no value is added to them or the oversight body by making them sit through a repeat training. Making a professional redo something they adeptly know grossly wastes resources, disrespects time, and insults ability. Allow opportunity for individuals to show proficiency, officially recognize their proficiency, and then let them go do productive work.

For students, this angle on waste of knowledge appears in reteaching curriculum or enrolling students in the wrong class. Take special note: The difference between engaging prior knowledge/reviewing content and reteaching curriculum is that the first two activities add value in the learning process while the latter does not. Activating prior knowledge opens the correct mental folder for a student to access previous knowledge and apply it in new learning scenarios. Review solidifies previous study and reinforces long-term retention.

Reteaching curriculum already mastered inhibits a student from moving ahead in the learning process. Recall the ideal state, when in every school moment, a student steadily and consistently works through skill, understanding, and knowledge acquisition. The waste of knowledge traps students as they are forced to remain mentally idle and "relearn" what they already know.

Practical solutions to avoid this pitfall include placement tests, differentiated playlists (see Chapter 17), optional reviews, and purging outdated/retired curriculum. Teachers must honestly evaluate teaching time earmarked as review and prior knowledge. Does it add value or is it simply disguising a waste of knowledge? I got caught in the "this is how I have always done it" trap while teaching Chapters 1-2 in honors chemistry, dragging the students through two weeks of density, units, and metric system review.

The students repeatedly saw these topics in elementary and junior high schools. Why was I doing it again? Had they not mastered the concepts in the last six years?

So, I pared the topics down to a true review and engaged prior knowledge, only using two days instead. Students then take a quiz to confirm mastery and move on. Students who lack proficiency are given videos and assignments as part of their differentiated playlist because they genuinely need to relearn the material. They can retest at any time to prove proficiency. The moral of the story? Scrutinize and honestly categorize reteaching as review/prior knowledge engagement or as a waste of knowledge. Respond accordingly so you always add value to students' learning experience.

Students enrolled in the wrong class also produces a terrible waste of knowledge. This goes two different directions: students not prepared for a given class or students overqualified for a class. Picture the student resting their chin on their knuckles, eyes glazed over, bored out of their mind because the class is too easy. Now picture the student with a quizzical brow, confused, and near hyperventilation because they are completely overwhelmed. Both scenarios waste students' knowledge.

In teaching three different levels of science, I often see this at the beginning of the school year. Through a pretest, observation, and discussion with students, I shuffle kids from honors to AP, or general to honors, and vice versa. It is tricky getting students in the class that optimizes learning at their current level but worth it. The first line of defense is the counseling office. Print a cheat sheet differentiating classes for counselors to reference as they enroll students. Include prerequisites, amount of homework time, course description, and key questions to ask a student and parent. Next, clearly communicate expectations, time commitment, requirements, and benefits of a class on the first day of school. Offer after-school availability to discuss class options. Then in class, keenly observe students for placement through the first week of classroom participation, questions, and homework completion. Teachers, as experts, typically read students well and identify best fits quickly. Then, boldly and kindly, encourage students to join the class that offers the most value at their current academic level.

Just remember, the first enemy of knowledge is lack of access. Important information remains unknown to teachers and students. Combat this waste through a sharing, organized, and communicative culture. The second nemesis of knowledge forces competent people to repeat what they previously learned. Honestly evaluate what information adds value to student learning. Ultimately, guard against lost opportunities for learning or reconstructing existing knowledge. Here is a rapid-fire list of situations that create knowledge waste.

- Creating something that already exists
- Not collecting student performance data
- Not using student performance data to inform instruction
- The goal is not measured
- Not sharing data between teachers, PLCs, or departments
- Procedural mistakes due to lack of communication or transparency
- Participating in repeated training
- Reteaching students content or skills already mastered
- Teaching obsolete curriculum
- Placing students in the wrong class for ability

Chapter 11: Be the Best You

Think of a moment when you did something well. You helped someone, shared information, encouraged a student, solved a problem, or accomplished a goal. It felt good…satisfying! Posture straightens, gait widens, and a smile fills your soul because your gifts helped someone. This chapter continues the theme of utilizing and balancing people's strengths through eliminating wastes of talent and capacity.

Talent

When we don't use or develop the skills, strengths, or passions of an individual, their talents are wasted. This applies to each person in the educational system, from the superintendent to the preschool child. Every person on the planet possesses natural gifts and abilities. They grow with exploration and honing and are further perfected through use and sharing. An English teacher told me early in my career that the best teachers teach in their style with their personality. She was telling me to use my talents to make my classroom look different from any other teacher's. The same notion applies to all teachers and each student. Every student's learning path bends and curves differently, according to their abilities and talents. The more we can use people's talents, the greater the work and learning experience.

The waste of talent surfaces in four areas:

- Requiring permission
- Professionals doing non-professional work

- Under or overutilizing people's talents
- Not soliciting or using people's ideas

Permission

Permission requirements for basic tasks eat away at an individual's ability. Teachers encounter this obstacle when they have to get permission from a committee, administration, or district to make mundane decisions. Examples include administrative signatures to purchase common school supplies, approval to order club T-shirts, tracking the number of copies made, or requiring a third-party presence for one-on-one tutoring. Inherent in a teacher position is a standard of trust, professionalism, and ability. Reevaluate the need for these permissions and determine if they truly necessitate oversight. Allowing educators to take ownership of their position honors their professionalism and relieves governing bodies from wasting their energies, too.

Students run into permission wastes when prevented from moving forward. For instance, the waste happens if I were to tell students to only complete the first two questions and then wait to move on. Really? Why would I need to give permission for students to continue problem sets if they understand the content? But how many teachers get hung up on this? Instead, allow a student with high STEM aptitude to complete a math assignment while the math teacher lectures. Great! The student's talent is utilized in an efficient manner, and the teacher focuses on students needing additional help. Keep the learning momentum going.

Procedural permission also wastes students' and teachers' talent. This includes teachers tracking down administrators or secretaries for signatures confirming basic tasks completed, like grades submitted, keys turned in, or a supply order filled. Students asking to use common supplies (scissors, stapler, crayons, wipes) or requesting consent for fundamental hygiene (washing hands, cleaning a cubby, sanitizing a desk) wastes talent of the minor and adult. In younger grades, a few of these may be appropriate. With training and practice, however, students can be trusted to take responsibility for such tasks.

At the high school level, a dear colleague modeled this practice. He showed that high school students do not need permission to use the restroom. The solution, a mole figurine (small rodent — this is a chemistry joke for those who get it) sits in a basket in the back of his room. Students grab the mole and quietly leave the room to go to the restroom. Students may only leave when the mole is available. No one asks permission and the class continues without interruption when someone exits. It's time to think about other tasks in which students can take ownership and skip needless permission.

Professionals Doing Non-professional Work

This is a "numbers game" that private industry guards but public education has overlooked. Do some math with me. Say a teacher with a bachelor's degree earns $30 per hour. Their expertise and job description are for fifth grade elementary education. Their position is skilled and specific and select few can replace them. Their time, energy, and talents should therefore be focused on instructing 10-year-old children. That is why they are paid $30 per hour.

This teacher designs an outstanding reading packet for the next term and then stands in front of a copy machine for two hours assembling packets. Two hours of their talent and $60 of pay were wasted. Photocopying does not require a bachelor's degree or specific teaching skill. A school aide, paid $12 per hour, can produce the packets with equal competence. The aide's talent is appropriately utilized in manufacturing the resource, costing the school $24, or 40% the cost of the teacher.

The teacher's talent is in the creation of the packet because they are a professional educator with specialized education. The aide's job is physically constructing the packet because they are a non-professional and paid accordingly. This does not mean one person is better than the other, like I said, it is a numbers game to maximize talent. As much as possible, allow professionals to do professional work and non-professionals to do the non-professional work for the professionals. Financial wisdom dictates the necessary hiring of non-professionals in a school to support professionals. Teachers can also find non-professional help outside of district and school employees. Engage the assistance of parents and students. Elementary teachers are especially good at organizing parent volunteers. Identify non-professional tasks in the classroom, then brainstorm ways to develop parent or grandparent support. Granted, some school locations are more conducive to family support than others. Reach out to city councils for "adopt a classroom" volunteer programs.

Students are amazing worker bees; what they can do surprised me! My biggest hurdle involving student help was my own letting go and allowing students to do things. Through experimentation and coaching, I developed student jobs to cover non-professional tasks. Obvious student work includes cleaning up after activities, straightening/wiping desks, and maintaining supply stations. How about organizing reading corners, alphabetizing math folders, or self-recording grades? Even at young ages, students can effectually complete classroom tasks. The responsibility and life skills grow student talent and reserve teacher talent for professional activities.

I was pleased when the district created a special class for me called "Para-Instructor." I got the idea from a wonderful AP chemistry teacher in a neighboring district. Students who passed AP Chemistry as juniors enroll in this class as a senior. They prepare labs, maintain equipment, track data, do data entry, tutor, and even teach chemistry classes in the absence of a teacher for the entire chemistry PLC (over 500 students, 3 teachers, and 17 classes). Talk about amazing. I write glowing letters of recommendations for these young people, and they walk away with marketable skills. Student talent grows and chemistry PLC teachers are freed to invest professional skill in chemical education. The bottom line is to protect professional talent and resources and, in the process, develop the talents of others.

Under or Overutilizing Talent

There are two sides to this coin. Underutilized talent occurs when there is little opportunity or willingness to share. Poor communication and jumbled organization channels compound this problem. Likewise, when someone is shy or uncomfortable sharing their gifts, they, too, hide their talents and, therefore, waste them.

The best remedy for underutilized talent is a culture that celebrates, encourages, and grows talent. Our dear family friend, Pastor Ron Keller, is the very best at encouraging people's talents. He loves people and wants them to use their gifts. Are you good with money? Teach a financial class at Wednesday family nights. You have a heart for people facing hunger? Open a food pantry in the church. You have never done that before? No worries, he will help you. He plants any seed of interest or ability in tended soil, waters it, and watches it grow.

Imagine a work environment like this; imagine a classroom like this. The premise is that the success of one does not take away the success of another; all successes benefit the whole group. Everyone is on the same team. Discovering and developing talent in other people catches like fire. Open the door of opportunity and people begin to spread fledgling wings to use their gifts — educational professionals and students alike.

During the last two years in our science department, we saw several teachers leap and share their talents. One teacher passionately protects the environment, standing as the inhouse expert on the Great Salt Lake (GSL). She designed a new semester course called Environmental Chemistry that is all about the GSL. The students grow brine shrimp, make salinity meters, and collect actual samples from the GSL on a field trip. I want to take the class! Another newer teacher loves organic chemistry, so he designed a class with all kinds of cool O-Chem activities and experiments. Another veteran teacher birthed a fantastic, hands-on zoology class, and yet another brilliant teacher designed a physics class especially for our high-functioning special education students. The teachers were given liberty to use their talents and try something new. With teachers on fire, gifts blazing, who really benefits? The students!

Fostering student talent is just as important. Allowing choice in activities, projects, or assignments can encourage talent growth. My personal joy is watching students discover interest and ability in different topics. Many students enter my class with no clue about the nuances of chemistry. When their eyes gleam during experiments or their satisfaction beams after successfully completing a problem, their talent begins to emerge. When teachers inspire a group of students to pursue a certain field of study, it's because talent matured under their care. The beauty of instructing young people is nurturing gifts already there and helping them discover new ones.

Overutilized talent happens when an expert helps others so often that they cannot get their own work done. For example, when an Excel, tech-savvy teacher has a line of teachers waiting for help. Or a favorite counselor must manage a constant que of students and parents because everyone wants to work with that counselor. Students also understand this; they habitually go to one girl in the classroom for homework help, so everyone wants to sit at her table.

How can we change this? A couple of ways to prevent overuse of talent are to first, set boundaries, and second, duplicate those talents. The tech guru teacher sets a time when they are available to help staff. To ensure no waste of talent, the boundaries are clearly communicated. The teacher then encourages two coworkers to attend a professional development Excel training so they, too, can support faculty in this task. In another scenario, the counselor surveys patrons as to why people fill their office so frequently. The counselor then passes the tips on to other counselors to help them grow their gifts and talents. Lastly, a teacher assigns peer tutors so the sole girl is not overwhelmed supporting others. Lean Think capitalizes on individual talents, using them in just the right amount, enough to grow the gifts but not so much to abuse them.

Not Soliciting or Using Others' Ideas

I came face to face with this waste of talent when we began Lean Think as a chemistry PLC. Success as a group depended on everyone having a voice, input, and decision-making power. I learned to let go and allowed people to shine, question, debate, explore, dream, and experiment. This meant we each needed flexible attitudes and hearing hearts. Many thanks to my team for the critical skills they helped me learn.

To begin, create space for the expression of ideas — everyone's ideas. Each person needs a turn to talk. Usually, one or two people gladly carry meeting discussions, but this doesn't mean quiet members do not possess valuable ideas. They just remained silent to keep the peace or because they have less assertive personalities. Be willing to specifically ask individuals for input; it will always yield gems of innovation.

Next, try new things. Say yes whenever possible. Implement experiments with coworkers' ideas as much as possible. The validation and respect elicited from enacting someone's idea is priceless. This builds team unity faster than any other action and affirms individual worth and talent. Overall, I discovered soliciting and applying ideas consistently produced a better product in each of our classes, more so than anything any one of us could have designed alone. The final invention embodied the best of all our talents — how could it not be terrific?

Likewise, students hold a wealth of useful and valuable ideas. I remind students I am the expert at teaching, and they are the experts at learning. I do not know what it is like to sit in my classroom desks, watch my instructional videos, or navigate my electronic calendar every night for homework. But they do! And I want their input on how to make it better, faster, and cleaner. The very best ideas I have integrated into my teaching practice have come from students. So, habitually invite feedback from students and reap unexpected viewpoints and rewards. Ask students what they enjoyed and disliked, what tool or activity most helped them understand content, and what one thing would they change if they were the teacher. Only their experience in your classroom can completely illuminate how to increasingly add value to student learning.

Purposefully look for ways to use and grow people's talents. Multiply the gifts in others to protect against overuse. Here is a rapid-fire list of how talent can be wasted:

- Neglecting peer or student feedback
- Not asking for peer or student ideas
- Insisting activities are immutable
- Unwillingness to try others' ideas
- Not recognizing strengths and gifts of coworkers or students
- Limiting opportunities for input
- Asking for help too late or not asking for help from an expert
- Taking too much time from an expert
- No opportunities to share talent
- Requiring permission for simple tasks

Capacity

The waste of capacity is a failure to realize the full potential in a student, teacher, or organization. This waste tends to be systemic and builds over time. The full benefit of an experience is lost, which then thwarts the maximization of a person's potential.

Students

In students, the waste of capacity is a product of multiple wastes over time. Student dropouts, below proficiency markers, no goals, or failure to dream are all consequences a young person faces when they are not reaching their full potential. Hearts grieve as we think of wasted capacity, as the faces of our struggling students fill memories.

I wish there were a quick fix to this waste, but there is not. The hopeful truth, though, is that something can be done. Teachers can make a difference in helping students achieve potential; the key is relationships. Many teachers enter education because they love children. So, that is what they do, love and care for students. It begins with calling students by name. Then notice behavior or circumstances and comment with genuine concern. Discover at least one thing about each student's life and ask how they are doing. Laugh, smile, and enjoy being with students. These actions communicate sincere care. Through relationships, bridges are built to help students grow as people and reach their potential.

Practical tools to combat the waste of capacity involve creating a bigger world for students. Encourage students to dream; what do they want to be when they grow up? Have students set big and small, long-term and short-term goals. Make students write or share their goal for the year or their goal on the next test, etc. Tap into interests, passions, and talents. If none exist, help students discover things they love in life. Coach students in metacognition, or thinking about their thinking. Encourage positive self-talk. Allow students to do more than they thought they could do. Provide opportunities for students to shine. If every teacher does this every year, more students will feel their capacity grow.

Teachers
The two most toxic attitudes that squelch capacity are:

- I can't.
- This is how I have always done it.

Growing and developing as a professional means change is inevitable. How many things I regret and, oh, the mistakes I have made — more than most! Reaching individual potential means fighting those inane mindsets with two uncomplicated words: try and experiment.

When wading into the world of trying something new through experimentation, make a couple of ground rules. First, give yourself permission to fail. Greater learning always happens from failure than success. Moreover, failure undeniably acts as a steppingstone in the learning process. I relish and celebrate fails in student labs. It creates golden opportunities for reteaching, example/nonexample, and misconception alterations. In discussion sessions, I tell misguided students, "Thank you! That is the No. 1, most common wrong answer. I love that wrong answer." Students have never felt so affirmed about a wrong answer! It is the same for teachers. Failure is simply another vehicle for learning.

Second, the goal is not perfection. When stamping out the word *cannot* and jumping into the realm of *try*, use the Minimum Viable Product (see Chapter 18). Design the smallest, simplest, most flexible solution to a problem. Launch the invention and then get feedback immediately. Fail quickly, make speedy adjustments, and go at it again. The goal is process improvement to incrementally become the best teacher possible and reach full potential. But do not expect to be perfect, especially when experimenting.

Third, let students in on the gig. When they know an experiment is in progress to help their learning, their grace more readily flows. Additionally, watchful eyes and attentive minds gather information to offer constructive feedback — because they feel safe doing so. This is yet another way to manufacture a team culture where everyone helps one another achieve their highest potentials.

The statement, "This is the way I've always done it," implies fear, apathy, laziness, or most common, favoritism. The beloved activities and projects teachers do year after year are the sneaky culprits hindering capacity. When repeating that sentence, pause and think: Does this thing I do over and over really add value? I

have witnessed teachers give up turkey bowling (I will not explain
— imagine your own version), six-week mythology reports, one-
month country reports, school dances, school programs,
fundraisers, AP binder notes, and playdough competitions. Any
one of these undoubtedly contained a degree of value, but not
enough to justify the effort required. As an example, our PLC's pet
project was the atomic snowflake. Teenagers, 15-18 years old, took
90 minutes to cut and color an atom that resembled a snowflake.
Sure, correctly placed subatomic particles littered the delicate paper
to justify some learning. The finale was that at the end of class,
everyone hung their beautiful snowflake from the ceiling. Yet, the
first year we implemented Lean Think, those small flurries were
one of the first, treasured projects on the chopping block. Why?
The return on investment for student time compared to amount of
learning sorely lacked support.

Systematic, intentional efforts remove the waste of capacity. The
mentality shifts from "This is how it is," to "This is who I want to
be." Both teachers and students embrace the challenge, work,
uncertainty, and vulnerability of becoming more. Even better, each
group helps the other achieve greater heights. Individuals allow
their full selves freedom to have an optimum experience in every
activity. Remove obstacles hampering a complete realization of
potential. Here are rapid-fire examples of how capacity is wasted:

- Lack of dreams and goals
- Students or parents do not value school
- School dropouts
- Lack of preparation for post-secondary training
- Untapped abilities, interests, or passions
- Not open to innovation
- Indifference toward development of potential
- Non-mastery performance and promotions
- Clinging to old activities deficient in value
- Attitudes of cannot or will not

Chapter 12: The Nitty-Gritty

I call the last three wastes of education the nitty-gritty. They address the semantics of academia and the inner workings of classroom details, like the flow, process, and requirements moving people, things, and information. The first of these three wastes is *process and handling*. Resources, both physical and informational, define the *assets*. Lastly, *defects* come as a result of errors in the minutiae of learning.

Process and Handling Waste

During the first seven years of teaching, I provided three signatures for every purchase I made — no matter how large or small. The receipt could read $2.50 for 3% hydrogen peroxide or $997 for an end-of-year glassware order. With receipt in hand, I filled out paperwork and signed on the purchaser line. I then walked to my friend and coworker's room downstairs for her department head signature. Then I made the long jaunt to the other side of the school to secure a principal's signature. Acquiring hydrogen peroxide took more energy and time than what it was worth. It was easier to just pay for it myself.

Thanks to terrific changes at the district level, all three signatures have been removed and no physical receipts clutter files. Each teacher bills student lab fees so they know how much money is available to spend over nine months. They purchase what they need when they need it, upload a digital receipt to the accounting system, and then focus on valuable teaching endeavors. Not one step or swipe of a pen wastes anyone's time. This waste of process and handling boils down to unnecessary steps or requirements in a procedure. The driving premise in Lean Think encourages the fewest steps with the most autonomy. Because process and handling in no way moves students learning forward, it must be minimized as much as possible. Examples of this waste tend to be concrete and procedural; however, abstract instances arise in the relay of information.

Procedural examples of waste include classroom procedures, regulations, or duplicated rolls. I visited with a first-grade teacher who stapled all student packets so the staple was perfectly placed in the top left corner. The students could just as easily collate four papers and engage the electric stapler as they walked into the room on Monday morning. However, the staple would not look as pretty. The real question is, does the placement of the staple add value? Now think about what else of more value could be done in those 15 minutes of the teacher's time or two minutes of each students' time before the first bell of the week rings.

What unwarranted regulations plague teachers? Printing term grades when electronic copies exist. Submitting meeting minutes no one reads. Software platforms that do not sync, creating a need to repeat data entry. What about procedural missteps that occur as faculty members simultaneously complete identical tasks. Do two teachers need to catalog department books, equipment, or supplies? Does the English teacher need to manage a book set or can the librarian take care of it?

In that same vein, consider students turning in both a physical and electronic copy of the same assignment or using a spiral notebook, composition notebook, and workbook all for the same class. Requiring students to use obsolete equipment or outdated technology. Students duplicating rotations with unclear rolls. How many students are acting as scribe in this group? Or worse, in collaborative work, a student sits unengaged due to lack of assignment. These scenarios cross into abstract process and handling waste. Communication and information are unclear, so the process flow becomes turbulent, repetitive, and unproductive.

Ambiguous directions or confusing expectations inevitably lead to procedural nightmares. Every teacher knows that a student left to their own devices will never choose the path a teacher would have chosen. A student only understands the need for certain instructions if an instructor explains them clearly. Even then, most students need the steps repeated or modeled! For example, when students ask me what to do next, I know I inadvertently created a waste in process and handling. My instructions lacked sufficient clarity, which interrupted the process from beginning to end. When students misunderstand expectations, it similarly reveals my deficiency in explicit communication which results in a handling waste. When I expect a minimum of three sources on a research project, I must publish and tell students as much.

Weak justification for misguided regulations and excessive process steps often comes from the "We have always done it this way" ideology. With an open mind and willing heart, consistently apply the question, "Does this add value?" Remember, more steps or requirements do not equate to "better." Streamline physical and informational logistics to the simplest processes possible. Here is a rapid-fire list of process and handling wastes:

- Unclear expectations
- Vague directions
- Entering the same grades multiple times
- Using antiquated equipment, supplies, or technology
- Creating a product no one uses (reports, assignments, activities)
- Students in a collaborative group not all contributing
- Multiple signatures or papers for one function
- Duplicating physical and electronic copies

Assets and Waste

The waste of assets boils down to two observations in a classroom. First, resources sit idle but should be used because they add value. Second, resources sit idle and should be removed because they do not add value and consume precious space. Assets also fall in either physical or information classifications.

An unusual example of a waste of assets surfaced the third year of my career. I refused to teach a sleek formula, the Henderson-Hasselbalch equation, in the AP acid/base unit. Feeling self-righteous in my pure love and commitment to chemistry, I insisted students perform calculations using a long hand method called ICE tables. My pride insisted that students truly understood equilibrium theory only if they mastered ICE tables in all situations. Then, in the third year I taught the tables, one of my brilliant students saw the formula in the book. Raising his hand, he asked why we did not use the easier formula. With pride, I defended my holy practice only to receive a quizzical, "Oh, really?" And he moved on. His simple answer inspired a sincere introspection and a reconsideration. So, I decided to allow students to use the formula and discovered they understood just as well. Every year since then, I not only encourage but emphasize the formula's use. Just as an aside, many of my students are smarter than me; I just happen to know more than them at this moment in their lives.

How often do teachers find themselves in an identical situation? A fantastic asset is right under their nose, but they will not use it because of pride, principle, or discomfort. For example, technology typically sits unused or underused in the corner of the classroom because of this reluctance. I understand, technology can have a huge learning curve and require big change. Technology and I mix about as well as oil and water. In the big picture, however, certain technology can add immense value to a student's educational experience. The return on investment is worth the effort to learn effective technologies. Seek out an expert in the building for support. Of course, never implement technology for the sake of technology. Only technology that adds value to student learning should enter the classroom. Likewise, look with a new set of eyes at other accessible assets unused or underused. What are neighboring teachers exploiting? What have students used, or what powerful tools could they be using that already sit in your classroom?

The other side of asset waste includes unused, misused, or continued use of obsolete items. Examples include storing old books you no longer use. Utilizing equipment more like a prop to set things on instead of its intended use. Students referencing encyclopedias rather than using internet searches. What about making general students use cheap colorimeters because only honors students get to use the "nice" spectrophotometer (no — I did not do that). Foolishly, however, once I had students use gumdrops and toothpicks to make molecules while beautiful molecular kits sat in the closet. What a waste!

The fear of possibly needing something in the future also keeps antiquated assets in rooms, which take up physical and mental space. Applying the 6S five-year rule supports purging unused assets. If something has sat untouched for five years or more, it is time for it to find a new home, either in the trash or a donation pile. Additionally, take time to reflect on when or where you use a certain asset. Now think about an alternate, available asset that better replaces the old one. If a newer asset comes to mind, then get rid of the old. For another trick, I imagine where I would go to create an activity. Is my first stop the old asset? No. Time to give away the old and allow room for the new.

As an illustration, a set of lab reference books lined the front shelf of my room. Not a single time did students crack open even one of those books. Why? Students prefer to find the identical information using a simple internet search. Why were those books still there? Because I felt guilty donating the manuals. I had spent classroom money on them, so I kept the books as penance for their lack of use. It took seven years, but I finally came to my senses. I admitted the lab reference purchase failure and then reclaimed some of my precious, limited shelf real estate. Freeing the classroom of obsolete, unused, overstocked resources makes space for truly valuable assets to benefit student learning.

Extend the idea of physical asset waste (i.e., books, equipment, supplies, or files) to abstract forms of asset waste. These include unread emails, papers waiting to be graded, or students not processing feedback. Notice the involvement of information and its transference. Information is a potent asset when used correctly. For example, emails contain information, but if you don't read them, then you waste time finding the (repeated) information somewhere else.

Student work and response to student work is a key asset in the classroom. Personal feedback on individual performance is priceless and necessary. No computer program gets into the brain and understanding of a child like a teacher. Student performance measures effectiveness of practices in the overall learning process. Without assessment, teachers move blindly through instruction. Assessment is an asset that informs teaching systems: stay the course, adjust, or remove to benefit students. Not only is grading vital, but timely grading is essential.

I remember a time two of my daughters submitted lengthy English essays in high school. Because the teacher delayed grading the first essays, the girls each wrote a subsequent essay without receiving feedback on the first. I can still hear their complaints after turning in the second essay, only to finally receive input on the first essay. They were both frustrated that they could not use feedback on the first essay to help them more on the second essay! It was an excellent wake up call for me as an educator. How timely was my grading? My feedback is an asset to students and even more effective when delivered at just the right time. A necessary extension of providing timely responses to student work, is students committing to read and process the feedback they receive. As mentioned in the grading section (Chapter 9), if students do not read or internalize teacher feedback, they gain no value. The asset of grading only moves learning if students use it. I require test corrections in AP chemistry to ensure students process graded responses.

Lastly, embrace this powerful fact: A teacher is the greatest asset in the classroom. For emphasis, I will say it again. A teacher is the greatest asset in the classroom. Nothing can replace a teacher. Sure, resources exist to support, enhance, and expand efforts, but no other asset or combination of assets replaces the effective teaching by an educator. COVID-19 proved that fact. Online learning can attempt to substitute for a teacher and classroom experience, but the same level of rigor, depth of understanding, or achievement is never reached.

Allow yourself to rethink who teachers are and what they offer in the classroom. View instructors, the feedback they offer, the instruction they provide, and the misunderstandings they redirect as the most commanding assets in a school building. With this attitude, educators take ownership of classroom learning, feel respected, offer innovation, and really … rock the world. Teachers are the No. 1 asset in education.

Just like the things targeted in the sort stage of 6S, wasteful assets consume precious physical space in the classroom and even more treasured space in a teacher's brain. Get rid of unused, outdated assets to make room for effective assets. It reminds me of my clothes closet. Why wear out-of-style or worn clothes when I have beautiful new clothes hanging in front of me? Give away the old clothes and enjoy wearing the new. The follow-up step in removing waste of assets is to embrace new assets. Education is dynamic as it adjusts to culture, demographics, technology, and student needs, so change inevitably knocks on the classroom door. Watchful minds recognize new assets and willingly walk through the growing pains necessary when implementing new resources to increase value for students. Finally, teachers are the greatest asset in the entire educational system and carry that responsibility with

pride, honor, and sacrifice every day for the students they serve.
Here is a rapid-fire list of wasted assets:

- Obsolete books, files, or equipment
- Old technology or textbooks
- Misused resources
- Overstock of supplies
- Unused or inadequate use of building space
- Space not optimized
- Student work waiting to be graded
- Students not using feedback
- Teachers not soliciting student feedback
- Unread emails
- Updated, new assets sitting unused or underused
- Lacking current assets
- Teacher not valued as most important asset

Defects

Lean for Dummies gives an astute industry definition of defects:
"Any process, product or service that fails to meet specifications is
waste. Any processing that does not transform the product or is
not done right the first time is also waste" (Sayer, 2012). Defects in
education primarily embody the last statement: processes not done
right the first time. When this occurs in education, the first two
industry descriptions result: The product fails to meet
specifications (measure,) and the product (student learning) is not
transformed.

Fundamentally, any action inside the classroom that does not
increase student learning is a defect. That hits like a ton of bricks
— effort with no valuable outcome. If the learning process is not
executed right the first time, then students do not score proficiency
in the measure. If students do not reach competency, it means
student learning was not transformed. This summarizes all
educational defects.

One fine point should be understood: Purposeful reteaching does not necessarily mean there was a defect in the original process. Teachers experience firsthand how the brain works. No one masters content or a skill in one try. Teachers purposefully design an individual activity to achieve a certain goal. Fully aware of learning patterns, teachers create related activities to cumulatively build and draw students toward competency. Intentional lesson planning with many and varied learning impressions is a hallmark of good teaching practice. The deliberate redundancy, or reteaching, is necessary for true understanding and retention. A defect only arises when a single activity does not accomplish the teacher's intended goal. And when that one step in the overall learning process must be repeated, a waste appears.

Unfortunately, I have gross examples of defects. In my first year of teaching, the poor students only earned a 25% pass rate. Three out of every 4 students scored below proficiency (below a C in a general chemistry college class). I still feel bad about that. I did not accomplish, even after spending hundreds of hours, what I set out to do. In another example, our PLC pulled in a meager 37% pass rate for general chemistry students on our first SAGE standardized test. Obviously, more than one activity did not transform learning in those situations. Sadly, students moved to the next grade level and were never remediated in the chemistry they missed. They just got pushed to another science class producing more defect waste.

So, what is the fix for educational defects? Being watchful, creating formative assessments, and amending processes so the next time you teach the "repaired" version, they really learn. The ideal state says every step in every process propels student learning. Find the breach in learning through becoming aware of where you repeat teaching steps (excluding purposeful reteaching or reviewing, of course) and find actual gaps in understanding or even misconception. Seize the defect, remove it, adjust the process, and move forward. The objective is to achieve an intended goal the first time around. Touch it once and do it correctly.

Defect wastes also occur in procedural and clerical processes. The greatest procedural defect comes from unclear directions. Misinformation, missing steps, or confusing instructions create defects which ripple into wastes of time, motion, and talent. Whenever students ask me a procedural question, I know ambiguous guidelines created a defect. I've heard these questions: Mrs. Laub, where are the graduated cylinders? Mrs. Laub, how do I dispose of the waste? Mrs. Laub, where do I turn in late work? Thankfully, the wonderful benefit of questions is they pinpoint the defects. I need to post a sign over the graduated cylinders, add one last disposal step to lab instructions, and provide a link for late work instructions on my webpage. Other procedural defects originate in missed deadlines, missing requirements, rework, or poor quality of processes and products. These all apply to both students and teachers.

Clerical defects follow data entry mistakes, grading errors, missing information, lack of communication, lost records, or duplicated paperwork. Every term, I see it in students turning something in, but it is not on their grade in the computer. What a waste! They look at the online grade and notice something is missing. They think, "Did I turn that in?" Then they put in effort to email or visit me. I then send them to their basket to search for and recover the assignment. Once the "missing" assignment rests in my hands, I must find the correct screen and assignment to enter one score, one that should have been entered quickly with the other 35 student entries.

Do not let these detail-type defects slide. They appear small and insignificant but require more energy than they show. The case in point is my one missing assignment example. Oh, not a big deal; I missed one student's grade entry. How much time and effort did both the student and I invest to rectify that one "little" mistake? Minutes. Precious minutes when we both could have been doing something productive but were stuck fixing a task that should have been done right the first time.

Catch defects and fix them with first, communication, and second, process adjustments. Because teachers work with people, coworkers and students, communication needs to be verbalized, written, and repeated to decrease defects. Because students are young, I discovered they need multiple forms of communication to alleviate defects. Every day the agenda for my class is written on the front board, posted on my webpage, and I literally read it to the students at the beginning of class. Important things, like the last day for term work, are written and spoken several days.

Even with open and clear communication, teachers inevitably get questions on procedural steps because students were not paying attention. This is a different issue. Consistently redirect students when they ask questions. I will say, "Did you look at the agenda on the board?" "Please go to the webpage and find the assignment you missed when you were absent," or "Ask your neighbor." I know many teachers effectively use "Ask three before me." (Ask Yourself, Look Around, and Ask a Friend.) A significant percentage of teaching efforts mentor students in life skills. Acquiring information responsibly is a powerful life skill. If students should know a procedural answer, do not give it to them when asked. Coach them how to find it themselves.

To get help with amending processes, solicit feedback from students on the clarity of directions. Students give excellent ideas on what to include or amend in instructions because they are the ones needing to interpret and apply them. Steps that seem intuitive or obvious to a teacher may be completely unknown to students. Ask students what would increase the clarity of instructions. Additionally, pay close attention to the procedural questions they ask.

With coworkers and colleagues, share routines for clerical work and habitual classroom procedures. Draw on the innovative ideas of fellow experts to remove defects. Lastly, let individuals set deadlines for their own projects. For instance, a teacher in the PLC is going to rewrite Test 2 for the team. Let the teacher decide when they will email the initial draft to everyone. I discovered if someone sets their own date, they are more likely to meet the deadline. Also, type the date set by the teacher in the meeting minutes and email the document to everyone in the group with a cc to an administrator. Print the date on future meeting agendas as a reminder for all.

To sum up, defect wastes occur in educational, procedural, and clerical processes. At the very root, a defect is anything that is not done right the first time. Educational defects stifle student learning. When a student's education process is riddled with defects, the measure will not show proficiency. Procedural and clerical errors derive from unclear information and process gaps. But the good news is that all defects will disintegrate with vigilant attention to identify wastes and a willingness to adjust processes. Here is a rapid-fire list of examples of defects that contribute to waste:

- Rework
- Documents with errors
- Omission of information
- Repeating teaching steps
- Inaccurate data or correcting data
- Not completing specified curriculum
- Below proficiency student markers
- Late work
- Missed deadlines
- Poor quality in work or product

PART III: Lean Think Tools

Lean Think

Chapter 13: Absolute Favorites

Now begins what I think is the best part of Lean Think — the tools! These equip teachers with practical skills and a mindset to take the terrific things already happening in a classroom and make them even better. The tools sharpen, hone, refine, and improve practices. They also aide in activity creation and curriculum design. When developing new resources, they help teachers make a stronger product on the first try. Like cooking in the kitchen or working on a car, with the right tools the job is easier, and the product is superior. The same is true for education. Lean tools fill a teacher's toolbelt to generate skillful, innovative, functional, efficient, effective, and robust classroom resources and practices.

As a reminder, implement tools after waste is removed. Using tools is the baby step after waste removal! Two cornerstone tools lay a solid foundation for overall course design: Load Leveling and Standardization (See Chapter 14). Coaching Lean Think fundamentals, I always begin with these. All other tools incorporate and build on this groundwork. Together, these two tools shape and frame an entire class. Load leveling looks like curriculum mapping with some tweaks and fine-tuning. Standardization utilizes brain theory to optimize repetitive tasks. With a firm understanding of incremental process improvement and thorough recognition of waste, Lean Think tools help construct the best classroom possible.

Load Leveling

Load leveling means doing about the same amount of work and applying about the same amount of energy at any given time. It is divided into three distinct levels: year, unit/project, and day. Additionally, three facets act as filters in load leveling design: workload (time and energy), content difficulty, and stress level. By evaluating teaching moments by workload, content rigor, and degree of stress, a teacher can evenly spread curriculum over time. This ensures both the teacher and students do about the same amount of work with the same level of difficulty at any given moment. To illustrate this principle, picture the following manufacturing example.

A mid-size manufacturing company requires significant amounts of energy for production. However, not every step in the process pulls large amounts of electricity. The company collects data, plotting power consumption over time in a kaizen study. Most often, the amount of power being used is steady and consistent. However, periodic spikes in power usage arise as well as surprising dips — intervals when less power is consumed. Of course, the manufacturer is charged a higher electric rate during power spikes.

The goal is for power usage to be consistent at any moment in the day even though some steps require much more energy. The solution? The company engages industrial-size batteries and an industrial control panel (electronic circuitry designed to turn systems on and off based on input). The panel turns batteries and electric company power on and off according to its design. The batteries charge in the energy dips when processes require less energy. The batteries turn on when other processes require large amounts of power, minimizing the spike of energy needed from the power company. This *leveled* the energy load consumption by utilizing power dips to charge batteries and decreased electric company use during spikes through batteries. Education sees similar dips and spikes in workload, rigor, and stress. I use the word *spike* to mean more required resources for classroom experience, and *dip* means fewer required resources for classroom experience.

Every content and grade level contains especially challenging topics and easier topics. Examples include, second graders learning the silent "e" in language arts, fifth graders being introduced to algebraic variables, sixth graders performing long division, eighth graders differentiating between primary and secondary sources in social studies, 10th graders playing the Circle of Fifths in band, or 12th graders applying acid base equilibrium to titrations. Each of these learning experiences represent a "spike on power consumption." They require more mental energy, time, and practice than other concepts. Load leveling first tackles these bumps in learning by looking at an entire year's worth of content.

Year

The first Lean Think tool I give teachers is load leveling the year. Some teachers naturally do this, but I discovered even veterans in the classroom can take another look at the year's calendar. Visually spread out the year's curriculum, whether this is written in a book or on 3x5 cards. Next, count the teaching days in the school year. Now begin filling in the days with the curriculum. As the expert in the classroom, hypothesize where the dips and spikes happen in learning. What will take a day more or a day less to learn? My courses typically have approximately 20 units with 90 teaching days. Each unit gets 4-5 teaching days: 2-3 days for lecture (demonstrations, group work, discussion, and direct instruction), one full lab day, and one test day with a springboard into the next unit. Harder units take the 5-day slots and easier units take 4-day slots.

I have load leveled six courses in the last 10 years and found this to be the most efficient method. Hesitant teachers, however, express concern over flexibility for reteaching and unexpected school schedule changes. Build in the wiggle room. Allocate 1-2 days a term for spontaneous time invasions. If the time is unused at the end of the term take those "free" minutes and add more value to the student experience through additional review, extension, or application learning.

Some teaching styles prefer to ebb and flow with the new, yearly demographic and impulse of personality. That is fine. Create the outline of the load leveling and simply insert the unit flavors you choose for the year. I see this happen often in English literature classes. Block out the units to do about the same amount of work and rigor over any given time, then juxtapose the new book choices. Try out the load leveling, evaluate student performance, probe the amount of value added, and adjust accordingly.

Like everything in the classroom, load leveling is an experiment. Teachers constantly collect data mentally and officially to identify areas for incremental, process improvement. I made significant changes to my AP chemistry load leveling after my first-year teaching. Acid base equilibrium notoriously stumps students — it is tough. My initial curriculum map "generously" allotted a 5-day slot to the topic. I quickly learned I needed to adjust and add more time; they were struggling mightily — some even crying. With content that was much too hard and a ridiculous workload, five total teaching/lab days were insufficient. I added two more teaching days, two additional lab days, and divided the test into two separate assessments. The added days came from teaching "dips." I used days from nuclear, organic, and solution chemistry because they are not directly tested, only referenced on the national exam. The content is still painful but now doable. The students put in about the same amount of homework time as any other unit. But it took experience to smooth out the homework spike of chemical equilibria.

As an aside, load leveling adds value to course vertical alignment. A fantastic group of junior high physical education teachers load leveled the entire three-year student experience for PE. By identifying goals, measures, scaffolded skills, and expectations, they smoothed the workload over the entire junior high experience.

From day one of seventh grade through the last day of ninth grade, PE value is cultivated in students through load leveled curriculum.

I also witnessed fifth- and sixth-grade teachers load level math curriculum. They discovered each group thought the other was teaching certain content while neither were. The sixth-grade teachers grumbled about unprepared students and unplanned reteaching days robbing current instruction. All the while, the fifth-grade teachers were completely unaware they needed to teach the content to prepare students for sixth grade math. Load leveling between the grade levels quickly clarified the situation, removed the defect, and added immense value to every teacher and student.

Unit/Project Smoothing

Vertical alignment and year load leveling represent the big picture. For this tool, work from big to small. The degree below yearly load leveling is unit and project smoothing. Again, consider the principle of load leveling and design each unit to embody approximately the same pace and burden as all other units. Do not make my mistake of burning kids out on one unit (acid/base equilibrium) only to have them bored and waiting in another (organic chemistry). In an ideally planned unit or project, students can expect a certain amount of homework with a given amount of effort similar to all past units.

I use the "boot strap" for unit load leveling. My units typically follow a two-week cycle. At the beginning of the school year, I get everything 100% prepared for the first two weeks of school. It would be as if a substitute were going to step into my room for the first 10 days of class; everything is ready. I pick one day a week to apply the boot strap. This year, every Wednesday during my prep period I do two things. First, I look at my calendar and lesson plans for the next week to make sure everything is completely prepared. Second, I examine the calendar and lesson plans two weeks ahead. I make a list on my electronic planner of everything I need to accomplish and prepare next week to be fully ready two weeks from now.

When the next week rolls around, I steadily work through the to-do list to get things copied, prepped, written, typed, set-up, and organized for the following week. I usually finish by Wednesday or Thursday. On Wednesday, I repeat the boot strap. I make sure I prepped everything for the next week and study two weeks ahead to make a new to-do list for the following week.

So, every Friday when I leave work, the next week is fully arranged and equipped for teaching and a new list awaits the upcoming Monday morning. At any given moment, I am a week ahead in preparation and two weeks ahead in planning. This allows for thoughtful load leveling across each unit. I have time to think, plan, and formulate student workload and content struggles holistically rather than rushing from day to day. Scrutinizing student energy and effort only one day at a time obscures the continuity of an entire unit, resulting in educational spikes and dips. Try the bootstrap. Move planning into unit chunks and watch success in load leveling take hold in student performance.

Day

The last and smallest increment in load leveling is the day or class period. Similarly, the idea is for students to be doing about the same amount of work with equal rigor at any moment. I want to avoid a slow start to the class with little to no value added, a rush and harried middle, and a lazy "let's clean up early" closing. From bell to bell, student learning steadily moves and progressively grows.

The previous two levels, year and unit, already set the stage for day load leveling. Deliberately organizing the year and unit provides the exact content to be taught each day. This maintains rigor, and the workload becomes comparable day to day. Review the content and mentally load level minutes in the day or class period. I do this as I write the agenda on the board. Additionally, in the morning, I do one more review of content, making written notes to ensure an equity in effort and difficulty within the 90 minutes of class time. Even with planning, the art of teaching necessitates educators rapidly adjust in the middle of teaching to avoid the excruciating spikes in effort or dreaded intellectual dips. Amend instruction throughout the time span so each student consistently engages a steady amount of work and rigor minute by minute.

Individual Perspectives

Three facets determine how to load level the year, unit/project, and day: evaluating volume of work, difficulty of work, and the amount of stress created by the work. Both teachers and students are considerations in load leveling.

Ponder the workload of teachers. Seasons of both peaceful and crazy amounts of work pepper the calendar. The beginning of the school year, end of term, and end of year commonly mark busy periods. The in-between times tend to be steady and predictable. For greater efficiency, however, load level a teacher's work. Ideally, a teacher invests the same time and energy on any given day, regardless of the time of year, but this takes planning and initiative.

To quell my busy seasons, I moved several projects to slower times of the year. For instance, I compile workbooks for both my honors and AP students. Rather than undertake the task right before school begins, I tackle it the beginning of every May. My AP students have taken their exam by this point, and honors students are finishing their last unit. Life is steady and peaceful thanks to AP test completion. I pull my master workbook copies, make slight changes for the next year, create a new table of contents, and send them off to the printer three months in advance. Registration numbers post in April, and from experience, I know to order 15% more books than I see on initial projections.

This transpires peacefully within a week that is not hassled or stressed. The print shop has few orders at that time, so the workbooks typically arrive before the end of school. They sit in the corner of my room for three months and wait until next school year and the first day I reenter. As I return to meetings and initial preparation madness, one large task is already checked off my list.

Giving ample time in advance for resource preparation alleviates spikes in teacher workload which decreases stress. It is interesting to note the direct relationship between workload and stress: The heavier the workload the greater the stress and vice versa. With my PLC, we shifted test preparation to at least two weeks prior to the test. The teacher writing the test has one week for design, reviewing teachers respond with edits within two days, and then the copy center gets one day. The test is in hand three days before the exam, giving wiggle room for delays and changes. If the test requires electronic design, then test preparation begins 3-4 weeks before exam day.

The sufficient time allotment allows for thoughtful creation and review without undue rush, overtime, and anxiety. Future planning and organization greatly aid a teacher in personal load leveling. Feel at liberty to shuffle projects to load level, even if they seem early. Remember, utilize the dips to curtail the spikes in workload and stress. A teacher need not absorb every crazy period just because it "comes with the job." Take control of the workload and spread it evenly over nine months.

Designing a course requires special attention to load leveling with respect to the student. From a student perspective consider their amount of work, difficulty of work, and stress involved. While moving through a course, watch the load leveling through the eyes of the student and obtain customer feedback on workload, rigor, and stress. Students need to daily do about the same amount of work inside and outside the class, press through the same level of rigor, and endure the same amount of stress. If any one of those indicators spike, teachers need to make adjustments by giving more time, shuffling volume of homework, adding teaching moments, increased encouragement, or additional content scaffolding.

In my early days of teaching, I easily fell victim to spikes and dips in student workload. I simply followed the curriculum, allotting days evenly across content. The piece I missed was student interaction with the curriculum. Some learning takes more effort and contains more homework which in turn creates more stress. Of course, other topics call for less of everything from students. As previously described in my acid/base example, I shuffled work and the time spent on different content to maximize the dips and minimize the spikes. In leveling the amount of work and subject rigor, student stress also leveled. The class became much more predictable, controllable, and manageable from the student's perspective.

Homework load leveling prevents students from having to read 20 pages with 15 problems one night and the next day hearing the teacher say, "We are at a good spot; no homework tonight." Instead, on day one, the students read 20 pages, and on day two, they complete the 15 problems. Or day one they read 10 pages and do eight problems and finish the rest on day two.

When a teacher builds more discussion time, provides additional hands-on experiences, and offers added practice so students have needed time and tools for mastery, they are load leveling. Academic rigor requires multifaceted teaching methods to aid learning. Leveling stress comes from care and awareness of student response to the workload, inside and outside the classroom. When students appear overwhelmed, the teacher should provide additional support to decrease anxiety and level emotional responses. Here is a rapid-fire list of load leveling ideas:

- Look at the amount of time a teacher spends outside of contract hours throughout the year — pinpoint seasonal dips and spikes
- For yearly "one of projects," spread teacher tasks evenly across nine months
- Assess teacher/student stress levels throughout the year and identify workload/content correlations
- Identify dips and spikes in teacher/student workload and after school time in correlation to different content.
- Minimize spikes by maximizing dips in workload, content rigor, and stress.

- Decrease time and effort allotted to content in dip seasons, and apply those resources to content requiring more energy in spike seasons

Chapter 14: Same, Same, Same

Standardization is my No. 1 favorite tool. I think it has the most direct impact on student learning. Standardization is a consistent method of doing anything repetitive and takes recurrent processes and makes them reliable and predictable. With this tool, a set work sequence characterizes the items and/or procedures that are standardized.

When I first say *standardization*, some teachers' eyes grow wide with fear. They think of the term as confinement and loss of creativity. Ironically, establishing standardized procedures in the classroom allows for more originality. The mundane hoops teachers and students jump through are repetitive by nature. When the "must-do no-value added" processes are standardized, mental space opens for powerful learning and ingenuity. In fact, standardization influences two significant areas of the classroom experience: habits and measurements. According to brain theory, habits open room in working memory for learning, and standardization establishes controls so process improvements are isolated in measurements. Creativity then comes from evaluating data and making inventive adjustments.

Basis for Measurement

Honestly, standardization is a fancy word in industry analogous to the word *controls* in the scientific method. Consider a terrific illustration using a scientific principle. A scientist designing an experiment requires isolation of variables. An input (independent variable) in a system wholly dictates a certain output (dependent variable). This occurs when all other factors are identical from trial to trial (controls). For example, I want to determine the perfect amount of plant food to give tomato plants to maximize growth. I buy three identical tomato plants and give one plant the manufacturer's prescribed amount of plant food. The second plant receives double the amount, and the third only gets half the quantity of manufacturer directed plant food. To ensure differences in plant growth solely depend on the amount of plant food, everything else about the care of the tomato plants must be the same. I take great care they each receive the same amount and type of light, amount and type of water, amount and type of soil, pot sizes, watering time, and air. Due to these *controls*, I can confidently assert differences in plant growth directly result from differences in the amount of plant food.

In a similar way, standardized practices are the controls in classroom experiments. An example from my classroom involves a self-efficacy experiment (belief in one's abilities). I worked for six years under a wonderful chemistry professor at a PAC-12 university. My teaching practices, especially in the lab, reflect his positive influence. I borrowed a clever teaching experiment from his classroom. A portion of his multifaceted, formal, and published inquiry required students guess their test score prior to taking a test. The results were incredible. Ultimately, students completed more rigorous chemistry and performed better on assessments by clearly understanding how well they were doing in the class (Casselman, 2017).

I decided to try a similar, but modified, experiment at the high school level. On the third test of the year, every student in honors and general chemistry wrote a predicted test score in the top left corner of their test. Once graded, final scores posted in the top right corner. If students guessed +/-1 point of the actual assessment score, one point was added to their test grade.

Surprising results ensued. Motivated by that extra credit point, students dialed into guessing scores accurately within two test iterations.

The best result was that it opened doors for discussion of, "Why did you earn a C grade — you even predicted it?" Rather than hearing complaints like that test was too hard, the test was unfair, or you gave me a low score, students took ownership for actions. We had honest discussions regarding study habits, homework completion, and classroom engagement. The chemistry PLC observed a bump in average test scores comparing self-efficacy tests to the first two tests of the year and test means from the previous two years.

This entire experiment was only possible with many firm controls in place. Every test contained the same formatting, each student received the same amount of time (barring our accommodation students, of course), each student had the same resources (calculator and periodic table), each student tested at the same facility, and the test questions were identical. If any one of those items had changed, the reason for the differences in student test performance would have been unknown. The test was standardized and contained one variable, students predicting their score.

This is an extreme example of standardization and how it elucidates measurement. However, standardization also allows for daily measurements through formative means. For example, quickly changing how students line up after recess or modifying how roll is taken in a physical education class is most effective if standardized processes already exist. Perform steps in a routine over and over, then modify one step. The resulting outcome change is directly related to the single process adjustment. Standardization pins the changed effect to a specific cause, namely, an incremental process improvement. Standardization sets the stage for improvement as it isolates the measured variable.

Habits

Habits greatly enhance classroom value. Obviously, they foster efficiency, but more importantly, habits free students' working memory for treasured learning. The more students' brain power is focused on actual learning, the stronger the educational product. Habits spare minds from wasting mental energy on commonplace actions. Instead, the effort required to think is protected for growth, development, and stretching. Creating habits has an upfront cost, but the back-end benefits significantly outweigh the initial investment.

Working memory is a student's greatest personal asset in the classroom. Understanding how the brain and learning work confirm this statement and show why habits established through standardization are critical in education. Working memory is housed in the frontal lobe of the brain. Imagine five slots where information can sit at any one time. When every slot is filled, working memory cannot process any new information. Every teacher observes full working memory when students' eyes glaze over: They have reached mental saturation. They cannot take any more information!

A full working memory must be emptied through a strategy called a brain dump, which shifts attention away from collecting and processing information momentarily. The current working memory moves toward the neocortex where it will eventually, hopefully, be stored in long-term memory. Brain dumps can be fast and effective. Simple tricks to empty students' working memory include: a joke, demonstration, story, song, contextual example, illustrative video, partner sharing, writing, stretching, standing, or a personal experience quip. I imagine the brain looking away from the working memory for an instant to focus on something else to empty itself and reset. After a brief joke per se, students reengage and once again absorb learning in the five slots of their working memory. Strategically watch for and develop brain dumps throughout active learning.

A teaching hack to maximize the five slots in working memory is to avoid filling the slots with stupid things. I do not want to waste priceless mental space with students wondering where the tape is, how to submit test corrections, when the lab is due, or what they are supposed to do after a problem set. I want those five slots open to attentively and enthusiastically pursue new thought, discovery, questions, knowledge, and application. Good news: The brain has a mechanism to guard the working memory from the humdrum — habits! And habits are formed by standardization of routine procedures.

The basil ganglia reside deep within the brain near the back base of the skull. This is where habits are housed. Habits do not touch, engage, or in any way consume the five slots of working memory. Recount the last time you drove home from work. What did you see? Probably not much. Your basil ganglia got you home using autopilot while your working memory processed discussions from the day or formulated plans for the evening. This stealthy mechanism allows for the ultimate multitasking. Repetitive actions are perfectly executed while pressing new thought simultaneously courses through consciousness.

Apply this to the classroom! Students move through ordinary routine seamlessly while preserving active learning. With habits, students do no waste valuable working memory on silly details that add no value to learning. The obvious takeaway is this: The more habits in a classroom, the more opportunity for real learning to transpire. This only happens by standardizing monotonous actions and items.

In hindsight, one of the most effective habits in my classroom is a standardized class period schedule. I have consistent schedules for lecture, lab, and test days. I remind students the day before which schedule to expect the next class. They also have access to the term calendar as confirmation and clarification. Lastly, because I standardized the flow of units, students can predict the next day simply from habit.

Visit any of my classes and you can forecast the following lecture schedule: The bell rings and I immediately greet students with a welcome, a smile, and a loving voice. I point to the left board to begin the starter whereupon I time the students. We correct and discuss the starter. I then physically move to the right board and read the agenda and answer questions. I ask students to get out notes and we begin lecture. Every lecture contains at least one activity (hands-on, video, demonstration, etc.). The students then practice what they learned by working with partners and guided teacher interaction. I wrap up the class with questions, takeaways, and final group discussion. Just before the bell rings, I give students permission to pack up and visit me with individual questions.

The best part of observing my classroom schedule is watching the students. Before the first bell rings, they have read the starter and have their notebook ready to write. When the starter is completed, their eyes move to the agenda before I take even one step toward the right whiteboard. As we wrap up questions from the agenda, students shuffle paper as they get ready for notes before I even make the request to prepare. Because of habits, my students move through the period, subconsciously prepping for each next step in the process. While their basil ganglia carry them past mundane tasks, I aggressively and purposefully tap into their working memories to develop chemical education.

Look for cyclical occurrences and frequently used items in the classroom; anything repetitive, predictable, consistent, procedural, or routinely used qualifies. Design process steps and expectations, then repeat, model, and reinforce them over and over. Push as much into the basil ganglia as possible to form habits. Do not waste one slot of working memory on thought that does not add value. Standardize everything possible to protect and optimize the student learning, or to engage the working memory exclusively for learning.

Work Arounds

It is important to remember standardization itself is not the goal. Student learning is the primary goal and standardization provides a vehicle to efficiently achieve the goal. Process improvement at the heart of Lean Think continually evaluates and questions current procedures. As such, teachers continually find better ways of doing things. When change is warranted, take liberty to amend mechanisms — and quickly. Standards are not set in stone; they simply provide a place to begin. They act as a foundation upon which to build and improve.

Danger lurks when standardized procedures lack relevance or updates. They must be scrutinized and remain pertinent; otherwise, unintended results precipitate: workarounds. A workaround happens when a different, easier path presents itself. They commonly transpire when standardized processes appear as an obstacle rather than a stepping stool. Students masterfully maneuver workarounds, and their shortcuts nearly always inhibit learning; workarounds remove controls and limit improvement because variables are unidentifiable.

When a teacher discovers a student workaround, two solutions exist. First, if the standard genuinely offers value, give the why and help students understand the reason for the process requirements. Second, unpack and appraise the value of each step in the standard. Then evaluate the set methods and ask the golden question: Do they add value? Ask the student why they chose the workaround. What would they change in the process and why? People routinely find better ways than prescribed steps in standards. Sometimes workarounds reveal the need for improvements.

I caught my students doing lab workarounds only to realize my grading standard was outdated. In several gravimetric analysis labs, students collected data by weighing samples before and after experimentation. Prior to discovering the workaround, I graded the student's final yield (mass). Well, the students were smart. They used stoichiometry (math) to calculate what they *should* have gotten as a final mass. So, in the lab reports, they recorded the values they calculated rather than the values they actually collected from the experiment.

The dishonesty in the workaround was wrong on the part of the students. But I had to be honest, too. I missed the goal. The point of the lab was for students to understand stoichiometric relationships between reactant and products in a chemical reaction. The students who fabricated their numbers understood that concept better than anyone else in the class. They had mastered the concept to the point that they could manipulate numbers to get an A. If I was truly measuring the goal, these students were earning A+ grades. Ironically, they had to cheat to get it.

What I needed to do was adjust my rubric to include participation points for recorded values, and grade written conclusions and evaluations for scientific explanation of the values they collected. Moving forward, I genuinely do not care what values they get. I just want them to be able to calculate values, understand what the values mean, know why they have errors, and understand how to fix the errors. With those goals for the lab, the measure had to change. But the measure could only change if I updated my grading process, my standardization. It's important to recognize when change is good for standards and to avoid workarounds.

Ever wonder why vacations are so exhausting? The answer: lack of standardization. In a new environment, working memory is taxed since there are no habits in place. Lacking familiarity and repetition, the brain constantly engages working memory, which is not so restful for a vacation. Similarly, standardization is a critical Lean Think tool that sharpens teaching practices. The beneficiaries are students. Establishing consistent, predictable methods gives a basis for measurement of student learning. Change one step in the process and the outcome directly reflects the adjustment. Develop habits to minimize mental effort on ordinary tasks and maximize working memory for content and skills. The important thing stays the important thing through standardization of processes. Strive to isolate small and large processes for standardization. The reliability of practices will develop a dependably high-quality education and improved classroom efficiency, while significantly decreasing student performance variability. Consider these standardizations:

- Create identical formatting for every test and assignment
- Standardize parent emails and newsletters
- Duplicate monthly calendar designs
- Run procedures over and over with the same steps every time
- Standardize shared work between teachers and classes – everything looks the same every time.
- Repeat the daily schedule day in and day out
- Consistently abide and uphold classroom rules
- House supplies dependably in their assigned places
- Respond consistently to repetitive questions. (Where do I find missing work teacher? ... Please look at the webpage.)
- Organize units with matching structure
- Model and then reinforce habits in the classroom

Chapter 15: Smooth as Silk

Wayne Gretzky, one of the greatest hockey players of all time, famously said, "Skate to where the puck is going, not where it has been" (Schuett, 2016). The quote emphasizes looking forward and anticipating future events. With preemptive action, current decisions can strategically intercept future behaviors, and Lean Think taps into these predictive powers with two tools: Flow and Just in Time (JIT). This means a teacher should look at movement of information, people, and things with an expectation of predictable responses. In doing so, they can get ahead of where the students are in their learning and prepare or design the path to keep students moving — smooth as silk.

Flow

Picture a car assembly line. Many visualize the old, black-and-white reels of the first Henry Ford Model T assembly line. Others visualize shiny 21st century cars whizzing down a conveyor belt. Robotic arms zoom in and out of the process, and people in moving chairs intercept each vehicle. Focus on the movement, or flow, in the assembly line images. Vehicles maintain a consistent pace as pieces and adjustments are methodically added to each car. Flow, outside of the factory example, is the movement of people, resources, and information without waiting or stopping. Flow eliminates anything that can prevent smooth movement. In the classroom, a smooth flow enables learning to move unhindered, which also includes the value.

I must interject a disclaimer: The first response to this from educators is probably some version of the following: My students are not identical (like cars) nor is education robotic (like an assembly line). They have a point, and it's 100% true! Education's product of student learning is much more complex than building identical vehicles. Because little multifaceted humans are the clay teachers mold, flow looks different in a classroom than in a manufacturing facility. However, the principle of flow still applies and enhances educational value.

Teachers know learning moves along as students ask questions, discuss topics, debate arguments, think for discovery, and experiment with manipulatives. None of those looks like a robotic assembly line, but education does progress in those examples. Simply put, a steady flow enables steady student learning without wasted time waiting or doing something other than learning. An educator, paying attention to this principle, will be able to distinguish between flow and waste.

Physical Flow

A practical aspect of flow is the movement of resources and supplies. What happens when students are asked to get out their laptops in a class? Are they talking, joking, or fumbling through their backpacks to find and finally boot up their devices? Clearly, this is a time when no value is added to student learning, and the flow of their learning stops. But they need their devices. How can teachers keep the flow going better when students retrieve or obtain any physical resource?

Consciousness of flow gives teachers new eyes for the continual movement of learning. Amend the previous laptop example. Instead, the teacher places a yellow laminated paper on the board that says Laptop. Through standardized practices already established, the students know to place their closed laptop on their desk before the first bell rings. At the ideal moment for a brain dump in the teaching set, the teacher asks students to turn on their computers and access a simulation posted on the class website.

Learning continues to flow without interruption at any point of the lesson, which means that value is maintained or even increased through this transition.

Student and teacher movement can significantly disrupt the flow of learning (waste of movement). In my class, the biggest physical flow challenge is mobilization from the classroom to the lab. Minutes tick away as students stand, grab lab notebooks, get safety glasses, and reassemble with assigned lab groups at chemistry benches. Zero learning happens in transitions. As mentioned in Chapter 8, my AP students begin in the laboratory on lab days, which eliminates the movement waste and flow interruption. For all my other classes, I strategically place transitions at a brain dump, and then I time students to make it more like a game, which encourages them to do it quickly.

A group of kindergarten teachers gave an excellent example protecting flow while managing movement of children. After recess, the 5-year-olds need a drink of water from the fountain, but the water break encroaches on teaching time. So, these accomplished educators have their students line up at the classroom fountain and do recitations as they wait turns for a drink. The thirsty students get their needed water *and* continued learning because the teachers figured out how to keep the flow going in this situation.

Informational flow

True learning and academic growth — building moment by moment — is one of the most significant challenges in education. Imagine an ideal 90-minute class where every second added value to student learning. Bell to bell, no interruptions or obstacles impede academic progress. Merely having awareness of flow, or a recognition of productive mental motion, opens the door for improvement to get closer to that ideal state. Enthusiastically protect the movement of learning and remove hinderances. You can push for simple changes that can enhance flow of information. For example, create a school policy that no school announcements are made during class time (only at the end or beginning of school), and don't make students ask for hall passes for bathroom breaks (See the mole example in Chapter 11). Standardized procedures like these reduce questions about logistics that breach the flow of education.

Andon Cord

Bottlenecks occur in learning when students do not understand something. It seems to them like the teacher is speaking a foreign language, and the majority are lost, which means the flow of learning is breaking down. Envision a class of 30 first graders going on a nature walk. They walk in a line through the woods while faithfully following their teacher. Coming to a stream, the teacher easily leaps across to the next bank. Shorter legs make for nervous jumpers, so in a matter of seconds, the students bump into each other, and the pile of youngsters stare at the teacher from the opposite side of the stream. What does the teacher do? They heave a large stone from the bank and toss it in the middle of the flowing water. Then, they extend a sure hand, and one by one, students use the steppingstone and teacher's support to cross the stream.

Every teacher experiences a version of this analogy in classroom instruction. Difficult content will stump the students, so a teacher will see lower proficiency marks or even confusion as the students' misconceptions muddle activities or processes. Learning was steadily moving through a unit, and suddenly, student learning stops and the class cannot move ahead until the hurdle is overcome.

In Lean Think, a way to halt the process in order to diagnose and overcome the learning hurdle is called the Andon cord, and the concept comes from the car manufacturer assembly line analogy. Along the assembly line, there is a safeguard called the Andon cord. Anyone on the line can pull the Andon cord to completely stop the assembly line. A safety issue, quality concern, or technical error warrants the Andon cord. So, when something goes wrong, a worker will pull the Andon cord, halt the entire process, fix the issue, and begin the assembly line again. Pulling the cord helps keep everyone safe and synchronized while the proper corrections or fixes can be made.

In education, both teachers and students can pull the Andon cord. For example, when the first-grade students stopped at the stream, they were pulling the cord, communicating to the teacher they were unable to complete the task necessary to move forward. So, the teacher fixed the problem by adding a steppingstone, and the students could cross in two steps rather than one leap. The same thing can happen in the classroom for many reasons.

My students pulled the Andon cord year after year when we hit atomic structure and introduced math to invisible entities, light and energy equations. Year after year, I coached, cheered, and coerced students to "jump across the stream" so to speak. I tried extra reviews and homework to help students understand and bridge the gap of comprehension, all to no avail. Finally, I found a "steppingstone" to keep the flow moving. A light and energy POGIL activity (POGILs are excellent science teaching tools) was the answer. The assistance students needed was literally coloring a rainbow with wavelength numbers typed over it. That one connection has made all the difference in flow for my light unit. When large groups of students with confusion or misunderstanding pull the Andon cord, they arrest academic progress for a good reason. It's up to you to find a steppingstone to assist them in understanding and continue the flow of learning.

Teachers also pull the Andon cord. Poor performance on an exam in an entire class justifies reteaching. The teacher pulls the cord by taking 30 minutes the next class to reteach and review missed problems. Students then complete a follow-up assignment to ensure comprehension. Only then can the flow of learning continue. With standard based grading in mind, consider building Andon cord days into load leveling. For instance, the Monday-Thursday lecture, activities, and assessments provide opportunities for students to prove student mastery. On Fridays, students who have not reached mastery receive extra support and students at mastery do extension activities. This anticipates students stopping at the stream's edge and pulling the Andon cord. Because the teacher prepared for the blip in flow, a steppingstone is already in place to assist students without compromising flow for the entire class. Here is a rapid-fire list of situations where implementing flow would increase student learning (value):

- Students waiting to get or turn in papers
- Mobilization of students
- Transitions
- Acquisition of supplies
- Strategically placing brain dumps during non-added value moments (transitions for example)
- Identify topics that stop flow of learning and create a steppingstone to keep learning moving
- Predictably pass information to parents (an email on the 1st of every month, etc.)
- While students wait in line do review or recitation
- Information and resources passing between teachers according to schedule

Just in Time

Just in Time (JIT) interconnects different disciplines of Lean tools. It is the homeostasis between standardization, flow, and pull (Chapter 17). Toyota views JIT as the synchronization between the factory and customer demands. The company produces exactly what the customer needs and wants precisely when requested. In the classroom setting, JIT balances the ecosystem of standardized procedures with flow. Moment by moment, a student receives specifically what they need when they need it, no more and no less. In the classroom, JIT is only making or providing:

- What is needed
- When it is needed

- In the amount needed
- To the quality needed.

What Is Needed

In curriculum design, teachers evaluate what is needed for student learning at a certain grade level or a given content. Course content fulfills state and district requirements. In my chemistry PLC, we mulled over two sticky topics, gas laws and nuclear chemistry. Gas laws are not included in any high school science curriculum (although they are briefly introduced at the junior high level). Nuclear chemistry is strongly emphasized in state curriculum. As experts in our content, we made two deviations to the state curriculum taught in our general and honors chemistry courses. Driven by a conviction to prepare students for life and to satisfy the JIT principle, we decreased the depth of nuclear chemistry and inserted gas laws into the yearly content.

By asking "What does the student need?" we made a choice in what added the most value to student learning in a high school chemistry class. I realize this was a bold amendment to the curriculum, and such a change should not be made lightly. In our case, it was after much discussion and debate that we finally diverged, even slightly, from the state core curriculum. Our students were still prepared for the final measure and achieved the overarching goal of the class. They did all of that AND learned gas laws because we deemed it was what the customer needed. As a professional, you must fine tune content taught in class based on what students need to be proficient on course measures, prepared for grade promotion, and successful in life.

When It Is needed

Timing is everything: Teachers need to know when it's best to give students exactly what they need. Even though I teach older teenagers, I quickly discovered that certain things should remain behind cupboard doors until they are needed. This decreases the temptation of distraction. As a case in point with my students, I keep crayons, colored pencils, and glues sticks hidden from student view until they are needed for a lab or activity. Otherwise, students (mostly the boys) are attracted to those items and cannot help themselves as they fiddle and joke with the art tools.

Two life examples illustrate JIT and the question of *when*. For instance, when making my husband a cup of morning coffee from the Keurig machine, I notice the water is low. It is the last cup that can be made without filling the water reservoir. Do I wait until tomorrow morning or fill it now? JIT tells me to fill it now. My husband likes to poke fun at me, saying my manta in life is "Do not put off to the next second what you can do this second." Doing the right thing at the right time always takes effort, but it pays off down the road. When in doubt, tackle the task now.

To balance that idea, realize that some delicate situations require patience and opportune timing. I estimate in the span of nine years, my husband and I purchased over 60 prom dresses. Our five lovely daughters are only six years apart from oldest to youngest, so we had between 1 and 3 girls in high school for nine consecutive years. It was so much fun — and expensive. In jest, I say the reason I went back to work was to help pay for teenage daughters: braces, wisdom teeth, cars, and prom dresses.

Being a wise and experienced wife, I carefully chose the moment I would set off the prom dress bomb every year in our household. I watched for a day when my husband had an exceptionally good experience at work, our dinner was delicious, and peace reigned in the house. When it arrived, I would gently inform him that we needed to purchase three prom dresses. I quickly followed with several store sale options and assured him we would optimize the prom dress budget money. He inevitably caught his breath, sighed, and then continued his evening with heavier footsteps and a little less sparkle in his eyes. Because of my careful timing, though, the bomb was more like a small grenade. Ask my husband what the best thing is about our daughters being in college, and he will tell you — no more prom dresses.

Careful timing can be just as helpful in the classroom. Simple things like students asking extension questions, teachers prepping supplies, or administrative email schedules are all handled better if the timing is right, but how do we decide when to deliver the information? Go back to the original goal: When would it add the most value to the customer? Your answer will reveal just the right time and when it is needed most.

I am zealous about delivering content at just the right time. A student may ask a great question, but it does not fit the moment in the learning process. So, I defer and respond with, "Excellent question. I will answer that in the next five minutes. Hold onto that question!" Sometimes I will write the question on the board so I do not forget, or I will ask the student to ask me again when I get to a certain point. For instance, "When you see me draw the first order rate law graph, will you please ask me that question again?" I have even told students, "That is a college level question! You are about a month ahead of me. Will you please turn to Chapter 8 in your workbook and write down that question? I want you to ask me that in four weeks." I understand the importance of building and connecting content which requires specific placement of topics. To answer a student prematurely without a solid foundation not only confuses 90% of the students, but it also short-circuits the questioner's learning experience.

Practical JIT situations arise in making copies, preparing activities, or creating assignments. Honestly, if I do something too early, I forget I did it. Then I redo it. The sweet spot for me is two weeks in advance. The bootstrap discussed in Chapter 13 helps me manage the perfect time to prepare for teaching. I work with an exceptional English teacher who prepares all teaching tools monthly. The trick is to find the best system to optimize when classroom preparations occur, given the unique personality, preference, and class.

JIT also applies to collaborative colleague work. When I was the PLC leader of chemistry, I created the weekly agenda every

Thursday. I had already completed my bootstrap of preparing for the next two weeks so I easily transferred information to our group work. I drafted an email with the attached agenda and let it sit in a folder. On Saturday morning, I quickly sent the email from my drafts folder to the team. My intention was to give coworkers time to process upcoming events and help them hit the ground running on Monday morning. After a year of Saturday emails, one coworker kindly shared that my correspondence stressed him out. He did not like receiving work emails over the weekend. Fair. I missed JIT for colleague information, so I immediately changed to pressing the send button first thing Monday morning. Everyone had one day to digest the information and come prepared for the Tuesday morning PLC meeting. Likewise, share information for students, parents, administration, and teachers exactly when they need it — not sooner or later.

In the Amount Needed

Students love to get teachers off on tangents. They think they will somehow have less homework or not be required to do as much on the test if they start a teacher rambling. I can fall into this trap, thinking student interest is piqued, but they are really just stalling. Be cognizant of how much information you give in a situation. Again, the just in time principle strives for the perfect amount of information or supplies in a particular moment to add the most value possible. Too few or too many resources are equally detrimental.

When sharing the class agenda during an April AP review, I will not tell the students about the STEM book report they will complete after the test in May. It is important information but not at that moment. The same is true with parent emails. Determine the ideal amount of information to give parents in the month of October. Or for faculty emails, include everything needed but consolidate to the bare bones — use bullet points with word concision. Consider the precise amount needed in supplies, time allotment, information, or requirements for a setting. Some investigation may be necessary to determine the right amounts.

The Quality Needed

This aspect of JIT especially suppresses recurring overproduction waste. In any activity, investigate the exact level of effort and resources required to provide the standard of quality desired. Remember, investing more energy or supplies than are needed to obtain necessary quality in a certain situation is a waste. JIT helps teachers deliberately design activities to acquire the sweet spot of resource investment versus quality output.

As an example, look at my extended family's gatherings. Both my mom and mother-in-law are wonderful cooks. When they host family meals, it is a feast, literally. Their spreads include the main dish, two sides, a green salad, vegetable, bread, dessert, and drink — at minimum. I used to do the same, until I became a full-time working mother and learned about JIT. The point of get-togethers is to be with family and enjoy good food. So, how much food is needed to accomplish that? What is the minimum number of dishes required to provide the quality needed? My evaluation enabled me to remove one side, the bread, and vegetable. Everyone still appreciates family time together shared over food. Removing several dishes does not diminish the experience; instead, I removed waste because JIT quality is spot on.

Now consider a school example. Ask these questions when planning an art project: How elaborate does an art project need to be to provide the quality the teacher expects? Is the project something to hang on a refrigerator at the student's home, a gift for a student's parent, a display in the library, or a portfolio piece? Probing those questions determines the amount of energy required based on the quality target. The portfolio artwork deserves more time, energy, and thought than the cute painting designed to hang on the kitchen appliance. Contemplate quality measures for bulletin boards, projects, labs, newsletters, emails, and reports. Identify the level of quality, then expect and provide that amount, no more and no less. Here are some rapid-fire areas to use the JIT tool:

- Breadth and depth of content
- Volume of supplies available to students
- Pacing and curriculum mapping: teaching exactly what is needed in the amount needed when it is needed
- When to prepare classroom work
- Number of copies
- Email content and timing
- Amount of learning in every situation
- Amount of homework
- How much and when information is disclosed to students and parents
- Level of quality expected in student and teacher work for various activities and projects

Learning moves as smooth as silk with thoughtful planning. The expertise of teachers allows for design that is several steps ahead of students because teachers see where the puck is going. They have tools and strategies in place to beat the puck to its destination. By the time students get there, flow continues, uninterrupted. They receive exactly what they need, when they need it, in the amount needed, and at the level of quality needed. With forethought of flow and JIT, movement through the educational process is smooth and continuous.

Chapter 16: Do It Right

As Lean took root in Japanese manufacturing in the early 1950s, quality became a central discussion. The overarching goal evolved to export higher quality products at lower costs to benefit global customers. More for less. As a result, Lean contains two basic emphases — *more* and *less*.

The *less* aspect of Lean Think is waste removal, to which a significant portion of this book is devoted. In manufacturing, less translates into lower customer costs. But in education, less looks like fewer hours outside of contract time for teachers and no busy work for students. Lean Think shows that removing waste proves the easiest and fastest way to improve processes and bolster student performance.

The *more* angle of Lean Think stresses quality. High quality in manufacturing boasts a superior product. In education, this translates into student mastery through the most efficient means possible. High quality also infers that students have a positive experience. I want both when designing my classes, which is true for a majority of teachers: courses that provide competency and a safe space for young people, but also inspire, develop life skills, challenge, and change lives.

Removing waste inherently improves product quality. However, Lean tools also equip teachers to purposefully sharpen and refine practices for increased quality. Two tools highlight how to design processes to build quality: Error Proofing and Jidoka.

Error Proofing

I have a soft spot in my heart for error proofing because it forces people to do things right the first time. I even create error proofing for myself — processes to force myself to do things correctly the first go around! In Japanese and Lean Manufacturing, error proofing is referred to as Poka-yoke, which can also mean mistake proofing. The word "mistake" lends a slightly different perspective, which can assist teachers in developing classroom error proofing. Innocent mistakes easily occur with young people, so teachers find ways to help students avoid common mistakes through error proofing. Lean Think defines error proofing as a device or standard that prevents defects. For a moment, relish the thought of students and coworkers performing tasks correctly the first time. How much waste immediately dissipates in that one image? A lot!

Life examples clearly illustrate error proofing. When a microwave is opened while running, it automatically turns off. A safety mechanism stops the emission of microwaves to prevent someone from being irradiated by high energy waves. A washing machine door locks once the wash cycle begins. This prevents someone from accessing the machine while running and getting a limb caught in the agitator. When submitting credit card information online, software confirms all information is included. Missing fields are flagged to inform the consumer to fill in overlooked boxes. Notice that these everyday error proofs have become standardized and common practice.

In my life, I have built error proofs which help me move through daily habits a bit smoother. For example, I put my lunchbox in my van immediately after I pack it. I make my lunch after dinner, simultaneously cleaning the kitchen and packing leftovers for the next day's meal. In the morning, rushing to leave for work, I often forget my lunch if it is in the refrigerator. So, having made my lunch the evening prior and placing it on the passenger seat of my vehicle, I do not think about it again until I grab it to walk into school. This only works in the winter months when the garage is cool. In spring and fall I put a reminder note on my purse that says "Lunch." Because I will not leave the house without my purse, I'm sure to read the note and prevent a hungry stomach that afternoon.

Notice I identified several common defects in my life. I am rushed in the morning and do not have time to make a lunch before work. Additionally, I tend to forget my lunch because of hurried mornings. The solution to these defects? A consistent process to circumvent mistakes. Preparing my lunch the evening prior guarantees food is ready. Placing the lunchbox in my vehicle (or writing a note) assures the food arrives at school. This same mindset applies to work. What repetitive mistakes do students or teachers make? Design processes to prevent the common errors you identify.

A behavior teachers rigorously try to error proof is cheating. Unfortunately, every teacher has a collection of cheating stories. Two instances of cheating in my classroom prompted new error proofing requirements. In one situation, a student claimed she did not like odd numbers. To her chagrin, she earned an odd numbered score. Prompted by her compulsion for even numbers, she erased five of the penciled X marks that her neighbor had written next to the incorrect answers. Her justification: The sum of 5 and an odd number equals an even number. (?) Well, thanks to this enlightening experience, all students now grade peer work in permanent pen or marker as an error proof against even number irrationalities, or cheating.

In another case, two polite and sweet young women simply "helped" each other out. They had graded several of each another's assignments and exams in the first eight weeks of the term. They averaged B grades on exams. While recording the most recent test scores, I was overjoyed to discover they both earned high A grades. I thought, I am reaching them. It is starting to click. I am a great teacher.

For accountability, I randomly spot check student-graded work. I wanted to relish in the victory of these girls' successes and pulled their tests for spot checking. What I discovered is they did not mark 2 out of every 3 incorrect questions wrong. When confronted, these girls responded better than any other students caught cheating. They owned their mistakes, apologized, and made amends. I flat out tell students caught cheating: I would so much rather they learn the irreplaceable lesson of honesty in my class now than after they submit erroneous taxes as adults. Always tell the truth! The error proof mechanism derived from this learning experience is students never grade someone's work twice in the same term. Students exchange papers with a different person every time they peer grade. Despite the occasional instances of cheating, teachers typically do an excellent job error proofing to help students choose honest actions.

Teachers also give strategic reminders as a common error proof technique, like when fourth-grade teachers email all parents a friendly reminder that permission slips are due tomorrow for the field trip. Or, when a teacher tells students that in years past, a certain topic is the most missed question on the upcoming exam. The teacher then works two similar practice problems to help them be better prepared. In another setting, a teacher provides three instructions for an activity. The students then write and repeat the instructions. The repetition is an error proof, reinforcing the proper process.

Consider various academic infrastructures teachers utilize for error proofing. Teaching all-state core curriculum builds a course guaranteeing students are exposed to everything they should learn in a class. This prepares them for standardized tests and promotion to the next class. Thorough yet concise instructions prevent mistakes because the clearer and more explicit student instructions are, the fewer the defects and rework.

In manufacturing, error proofing is utilized in planned and preventative maintenance of equipment. Maintenance programs keep machines running smoothly so processes flow uninterrupted. Likewise, maintenance in education takes the form of regular reflection and data analysis. Use numbers to quantitatively reveal student competency. Collaborate with coworkers to unpack data, identify weaknesses, and brainstorm improvements. Seek student feedback for fresh ideas from a different perspective. Film one's class to evaluate processes as an observer would. Choose times throughout the year to look at data and contemplate student progress. Select one or two improvements to error proof and create systems that encourage students and teachers to do things right the first time. I use unit tests, mid-term, and end-of-term markers as my moments for classroom reflection and maintenance.

Fundamentally, teachers who practice academic error proofing seek out mistakes and create procedures to minimize or remove gaffes. Through planning and preparation, quality increases proportionally as the frequency of errors decreases. Establishing practices and mechanisms that prompt teachers and students to do things correctly the first time polishes the high-quality product of student learning. Here is a rapid-fire list of error proofing ideas:

- Create and email meeting agendas before meetings
- Time meetings
- Time student activities and transitions
- Require pens for grading
- Frequently change student graders
- Have students write "Corrected by…Name" on items they grade
- Students sign for checked-out items
- Email reminders to students and parents
- Identify content that students typically struggle with and tell students ahead of time
- Spend extra time on difficult content and tell students why
- Reflect on data and student performance; look for areas to decrease errors
- Provide clear, concise, yet thorough instructions

Jidoka

Jidoka is a Japanese word Toyota created. It reflects the driving goal of quality and creates a paradigm shift in the way processes are viewed. It means "quality at the source" or "quality that is built at the source." The idea insists that every touch and step of developing a product must add quality. Quality cannot be "inspected in" at the end of production during a final product review. At that point, it is too late to add or increase quality. My husband likes to use the term "baked in" to describe quality. Once you make the bread, you cannot go back to add salt. The bread's quality and flavor reflect how it was made. Quality is fashioned as the product is formed.

This places the responsibility for quality squarely on the shoulders of every person who interacts with the product. The philosophy says each person has ownership and a duty to guarantee quality in their step during the production process. If an issue arises, they have authority and an obligation to fix it to protect quality. If they cannot fix it, they are compelled to stop the process (pull the Andon cord, Chapter 15) and seek help to rectify the problem. The product does not move forward until the problem is overcome and quality assured.

Look at this from the perspective of workers on an assembly line. They receive great respect as the expert in their position, so they have liberty to guard quality through decisions and actions. They also bear the burden to ensure quality at their step is top-notch before the product moves to the next step. This principle fosters a high level of ownership and responsibility.

Now apply this to education and wow! Every person in the process of student learning holds responsibility for quality education. This includes teachers, students, and parents. Obviously, teachers significantly impact the quality of education students receive. Research has shown this for years. However, students are also integral in the learning process; they participate in their education just as much or more than the teacher. Parents also play a substantial role supporting and assisting students at home through their academic career. When each player in a student's education takes personal responsibility for quality learning and lets nothing slide, education achieves a higher level.

Jidoka is understood through two phrases:

- Touch it once, and do it right the first time
- Accept no defects, make no defect, and pass no defects.

Everyone is responsible for quality, and quality cannot be added while a student is taking a final assessment because their level of learning at this point is already "baked in." The measure can only reveal the level of quality added at each step in a process. To ensure quality at each academic increment, every person involved must internalize the two phrases of Jidoka as a cultural norm.

Touch It Once

My grandma loved idioms. A product of the Great Depression and member of the Builder Generation, she valued hard work and resources. One of her favorite idioms highlighted this: An ounce of prevention is worth a pound of cure. She quoted this many times to me as a child. She was trying to teach me to take the time to do something correctly and perfectly the first time. If I did not, eventually I would have to circle back to amend my work, and it always takes much more effort the second time around. In her endearing way, she was teaching me to touch it once and do it right the first time.

Every time I must redo something, I scold myself and think, touch it once! This happens with physical, mental, and electronic challenges or mistakes. I walk to and from the filing cabinet only to realize, once seated, I need another file. So, I repeat the process. A better way would have been to pause and think, "I am headed to the filing cabinet, do I need anything else while I am there?" Sometimes just slowing down half a tick prevents mistakes and repeating work that eats away at quality.

Mentally, how many times has an issue rolled over and over in my head? I arrest the problem and tell my brain to stop it! I then take the time and energy necessary to work through the hurdle, initiate a solution, and calendar the follow-up. I do not have time or energy to waste on something that is already a challenge, let alone to allow it to absorb my limited mental resources. Looking from a different perspective, electronically count how many times the students boot and reboot computers. Or, log clicks going back and forth between windows (I love multiple screens!). Searching for files or information with repeated clicks wastes time and causes frustration, which robs quality. Possibly the biggest electronic violation of Jidoka is distraction. Students or teachers can easily be diverted by social media, news, a game, or other entertainment. Time and energy quickly evaporate in those distractions and the moment for productive work is lost. The student or teacher must touch the computer again to complete the assignment when it could have already been finished.

A result of Jidoka, I now look for things I do repetitively and create templates. For instance, I email parents on the first of every month. I provide a brief overview of content (Intermolecular Foreces and Kinetics), workload (two labs and two tests), and important dates (one holiday and mid-term). From year to year, many of the same things happen every month. I made a document folder called "parent email" for honors, CE, general, and AP chemistry. As the new month rolls around, I open that month's email template for a particular course, fix dates, reread to confirm applicable content, double-check nothing is omitted, and do a mass emailing. I created a November email that will be nearly identical to what I need next year. Why draft it again? Save the email and do it once.

Other templates I saved include recommendations and student/parent emails. At the level of education I teach, I write approximately 50 letters of recommendation a year. I am able to repeat sections of recommendations, e.g., course description, para-instructor responsibilities, etc. Additionally, personality or extracurricular activities can be similar between students, e.g., athletics, music, work ethic, or social skills. I pick and choose from different recommendation templates to fashion a unique letter for each student.

I also send many individualized emails in a school year. The emails teachers do not like to send are failing notices and citizenship warnings, so in my parent email folder, I have templates for both. My favorite emails are in my "good job" document. I learned this from a district teacher mentor my third year of teaching. Every year, I send at least one email to parents celebrating their child for something notable I observed in class. It can be a test grade, lab performance, random act of kindness, hard work, peer inclusion, academic improvement, or time invested outside of class. I shoot off at least five good job emails every Friday. It is a joyful experience to celebrate a student for exceptional performance or behavior in front of their parents. Because various templates are created, it does not take long to send either a monthly or personalized email. Both go a long way in keeping parents informed and boosting student morale.

The practice of touch it once and do it right the first time is taught to students through instructions and error proofing. Examples include the simple action of a student putting their name on an assignment, placing papers in the correct homework folder, or reading and listening to instructions. The principle must be overtly and verbally taught, though. It makes more sense to students when they know the why behind a requirement rather than just being told what to do. For instance, students put their names on their papers so they do not have to redo an assignment, look through a stack of no-name papers, or explain missing assignments to parents. If students do not do things correctly the first time, it's important to allow for natural consequences which will develop an appreciation for "touch it once." Nurture students to internalize the value that "an ounce of prevention is worth a pound of cure."

Accept, Make, Pass

Not accepting defects is a principle in Lean; however, there is one rare instance where I break from Lean. In manufacturing, if the product contains a defect when passed off, it is returned to the worker in the previous step. Imagine a phone manufacturer receives a shipment of cracked screens. Without wasting time, communication buzzes between a phone company manager and a screen company manager. The phone company promptly returns the broken screens while the screen company puts in a rush order to send out new and perfect screens to their customer. Under no circumstances would the phone company accept and pay for damaged screens. They accept no defects.

Education lacks such luxury. On the contrary, academia welcomes all forms of student learning (educational product). With genuine love and open arms, every child is met right where they are: brilliant, impaired, stable, dysfunctional, healthy, broken, cared for, neglected, fluent, ESL, happy, or hurting. Teachers within any given class accept diverse levels of academic ability and emotional stability. Through the amazing gifts of educators, each child moves forward no matter their challenges. The educational system does not produce a pile of identical widgets like manufacturing. The product of student learning is ethereal and specific for each young mind. The goal is to bring every student to their greatest academic potential. As a result, the final product looks slightly different for each person.

Certain logistical aspects within education do, however, warrant an "accept no defect" stance. For example, teachers must tactfully insist on up-to-date equipment and resources. Don't hesitate to use data to illustrate the importance of purchasing modern classroom devices. It is more costly not to buy the right tools for teachers and students than to equip classrooms with cheap or antiquated resources. An ill-educated individual from a school that did not have proper tools and school equipment will end up costing society much more than the small amount it would have cost to provide an up-to-date, quality learning experience.

Expecting quality work between teachers in a PLC or department resembles the "accept no defects" policy. Other examples include students coming to school prepared; principals hiring excellent teachers and counselors; administration and teachers helping to adjust student, parent, and community attitudes regarding education; and teachers requiring completed work. When feasible, accept no defects. Insist upon top-notch items and attitudes to build a solid learning experience for every child.

Make No Defects

Teachers and students are most involved in the "make no defect" section of Jidoka. The key is both teachers and students are responsible for quality education. Ideally, both constantly use incremental process improvement to add maximum value to the learning experience. Each persist to achieve the highest quality. Each pull the Andon cord when quality is lacking and they need to stop and fix issues. Teachers provide the best learning experience possible while every student pushes themselves to mastery.

But in reality, no one has reached the ideal state. Everyone is somewhere in the middle of the process, moving from the current to the ideal state. The idea of making no defects is another way for teachers to approach incremental process improvement. Teachers should ask themselves in any one step of a process: What can be done to increase quality and move students forward? Students must also be taught how to ask this same question. They need to learn the value and skills required to build quality. A delicate dance happens when teachers model learning then transfer the learning for students to take ownership. The principle of Jidoka is yet one more skill that teachers instinctively teach children: how to learn and how to think about their own thinking, or understand the metacognition of learning.

Pass No Defects

The idea to pass no defects most profoundly impacts vertical alignment. What students bring with them from last year's grade or content level hugely influences the effectiveness of the current year's class. The chemistry knowledge and skills I send with my students to their college chemistry classes will reveal any defects I passed along. Often students write to tell me they are acing college chemistry and were well prepared. I love that! It means I passed them with no defects. I thoroughly prepped them for the rigors of post-secondary science by building quality into their learning. What a relief!

In a smaller sense, passing no defects is a result of both teachers and students pulling the Andon cord when there is an error. When teachers identify misconceptions and do reteaching, they refuse to pass a defect from the current topic to the next. When students seek extra help when confused, they prevent passing a defect into the next step of learning. They arrest the issue and fix it immediately.

The practice of accepting no defects, making no defects, and passing no defects deviates slightly from Lean Manufacturing because education accepts all students right where they are. The beauty and challenge of education is that teachers (imperfect themselves) take imperfect little people, and do a wonderful thing, educate them. Additionally, the education process is performed with a focus on quality built by educators and taught to students. Educators and students work together to make the best learning experience possible; as a team, they bake in excellence. This fully equips students for the next level of schooling.

The reality of life is that no one has time or energy to fix something later. The most efficient use of resources, which embeds (bakes in) quality, is to do something purposefully and intentionally right the first time. Like the Japanese quality revolution proved, removing waste decreases workload and creates space to build more quality into a product, which in our case is student learning. Here is a rapid-fire list of Jidoka ideas:

- Make templates for emails
- Follow instructions

- Maintain standard processes
- Teach students the principle of quality
- Teach students metacognition
- Confirm accurate content vertical alignment
- Teach all course content for seamless grade promotion
- Mentally work through ideas and issues so they do not continually take brain power
- Do things correctly the first time
- Request up-to-date resources and equipment
- Build quality into processes through standardization and error proofing

Chapter 17: Transfer Control

Two tools in Lean Think focus on control. Rather than focusing on the traditional idea of taking control, Lean Think emphasizes strategic transfer of control. Questions of ownership and expertise steer decisions of control. It took me two years to figure out where the first tool of "push vs. pull" fits in education. When I finally made the connection, I unearthed a central tenet of academia embedded within Lean Think principles, which is students owning and taking responsibility for their education. The second tool addressing control is "Gemba walks." Both tools, once understood, are obvious common-sense practices, but ironically, they both go against workplace norms. Utilizing these tools assigns control to the correct party at the correct time.

Pull vs. Push

In a nutshell, pull is a customer consuming what they want at the rate they want it. For a student, the "pull" moves them through the learning process at their own pace. As a student masters one concept, they move to the next and the next according to their ability and speed. On the other side, "push" in manufacturing derives from the worker forecasting the rate at which a customer will consume a product. Push in education is the teacher designing curriculum at a pace necessary to complete all standards within a school year. The teacher also takes into consideration the predicted average rate at which a classroom of students can effectively absorb content. Education has used the push system for centuries; however, this generation of educators is beginning to transition from a push to a pull system. For the first time in history, education can institute pull because of new technological resources. The easiest way to understand this abstract concept is through the lens of manufacturing and classroom examples.

Two scenarios exist in manufacturing. In the 20th century, American car manufacturers, having great resources, pushed thousands and thousands of cars at a time onto sales lots. Predicting the rate of consumer consumption and estimating how many cars they needed to make at any given moment, executives fired up plants and wowed the world with huge volumes of vehicles. Toyota had a different approach. Contrasting the Western model, Toyota synchronized the number of cars produced with real time consumer consumption. As a car was purchased, a car was made. Notice the control of production in the two scenarios. In the Western push model, manufacturers control the amount of product made. In the Toyota model, the customer controls the volume produced.

These industry examples translate into the educational setting. I have used a push model for most of my teaching career, as have a large majority of educators. Take my honors chemistry class as the case study. Imagine a large sleigh, Mrs. Laub's chemistry sleigh. I welcome students at the beginning of the year and enthusiastically invite them aboard my exciting sleigh. I position myself behind the handlebar, lean with all my weight, and begin to push the students through content. The ride glides smoothly through metrics, chemical/physical changes, and density. Then, end of September, we encounter light and atomic structure. As invisible particles take on mathematical formulas, some students begin to fall off the ride. Undeterred, I steadily press forward with one shoulder under the bar, grab fallen students with my free arm, and heave them back into their seats. All the while, a handful of students sit in the front row of the sled shouting, "We want to go faster! Push harder. We want to feel the breeze in our hair."

Nine months, September through May, I push students through curriculum, juggling the few who continue to lag, the handful who impatiently desire a faster clip, and the majority who remain satiated by the pace. It's exhausting to manage all three groups, but I control the pace. By sheer force of will, I muscle through mounds of content until, with a sweaty brow and sigh of relief, we cross the finish line at the end of the school year. I am not alone in this analogy. Most teachers fire up their own classroom sleds at the beginning of each year, put their shoulders to the handlebar, and push.

Now imagine an alternate scene. At the beginning of the school year, each student sits individually in their own sled. Each student determines their own pace. A student consumes and processes content until topics and skills are mastered. The student controls the rate at which tasks are accomplished. Of course, this sounds wonderful, ideal even, but there is a significant flaw in the picture. Who powers the sled? In the first scenario, the teacher pushes the sled. In the second scenario, students sit in individual sleds. What makes them move? A teacher cannot run around and simultaneously push 30 different sleighs at 30 different speeds. Instead, the power for individual sleds comes from online learning and resources outside the classroom.

Some in education think students can push their own sled, the idea being students can learn from sources other than the teacher (online learning, for example) and with intrinsic motivation to maintain a steady pace of movement. Recent COVID-19 shutdowns, soft closures, and widespread remote learning revealed students manning their own academic sleds is mostly disastrous. Frankly, online learning cannot reach the same rigor and depth of learning experienced firsthand with a skillful teacher. Additionally, students, being young humans, lack internal drive and self-regulation to support a sound pace. But we already know the traditional push model is antiquated. The happy medium incorporates technological resources to support teachers so they aren't the sole power behind the academic sleigh.

My classroom sleigh analogy really describes the notion that education needs to utilize both push and pull. Everyone still gets on the sled at the beginning of the year, and I push. However, from time to time, students jump off the big classroom sleigh and get on their own personal sled. Resources other than direct instruction from me power their sled. Students who were falling off because the pace was too quick have adaptive resources from my eBooks. They watch support videos I created or complete slightly different assignments for extra review and practice on what they find challenging. Students feeling bored by my pace hop onto their sleds to zip perpendicular to the direction of the class. They take off on more in-depth learning within the same topic with the adaptive eBook or an optional lab experience. Otherwise, they zip ahead, park their sled for a while, and do other schoolwork until we catch up. Accelerated students can work ahead. When I teach content they've already mastered, they are free to enter our hall's common area and work on other homework. However, they must show me their productive, value added work from the class period.

The advanced students who achieve mastery before the rest of the class can still find ways to add value to their education while in my classroom. If a student mastered a concept quicker than I teach it, I have no problem when they use my class time to add value from another class. The goal is for students to have a positive experience and learn chemistry. If a student achieves the goal faster than anticipated, then please, go add value to another class.

At the beginning of the school year, I can give students the option to work ahead because 100% of my class content and assignments are available online. Surprisingly, very few students take me up on the option. My informal, end-of-year surveys indicate students prefer to work within a relationship and appreciate the benefit of my expertise with real-time teaching and question answering. They find learning more engaging and enjoyable with social interaction between their peers and me.

An overarching goal of education is to move students from a push to pull system of learning. The partnership between teachers and parents eventually equips students with skills to take full ownership for their own education. Using the push tool, teachers can model and teach learning strategies. Then, like parenting, teachers slowly and strategically turn the reigns over to students, choosing bits and pieces of responsibility to transfer. Because students are learning how to manage personal control and discipline, teachers allow for choices and allow consequences for feedback. With pull as the goal, teachers intentionally look for opportunities to teach educational ownership and put the control into students' hands.

Several techniques exist to encourage students to get onto a personal sleigh and pull their education. As is necessary, teachers offer more support and push at the beginning of the year than the end of the year, but throughout nine months, they deliberately plan handovers of control, through scaffolding, for students to assimilate and practice ownership. As teachers do this across grade levels, students consistently take more ownership of learning every year. Ideally, by high school graduation, young people should stand fully prepared to maintain and grow their future learning.

A foundational tool to help students develop pull is choice. Giving students choice in their learning experience moves some control from the teacher to the students. Situations that invite opportunities for choice include study strategies, goals, due dates, and differentiation of homework or assessments. For example, teach and practice study strategies during class time, then encourage students to choose the ones they want to use at home. Have students write goals at the beginning of the year, term, and unit. Check that student goals are specific, and measurable; make sure they have a timeline, the why of their goal, and concrete steps on how to accomplish it. Provide options for post-test work, e.g., unit test corrections, rework unit assignments, new problem sets, tutoring, unit quiz, etc. Offer different assessment types, like oral report, slide presentation, movie, written essay, or blog.

Allow students to choose when and where they complete homework, within reason. For example, my students have a hard one-week deadline every Sunday at midnight (a scaffold push tool). Even though I may see students three times and give three assignments within a given week, they choose within a 7-day period when and where to complete the work. Just because I allocate 15 minutes at the end of class to begin work and answer questions does not mean students must work on my homework. They choose. (They must work on homework, but it does not have to be from my class. They cannot play on phones.) As a result, they take ownership of decisions and the natural consequences that ensue.

Playlists

Playlists afford an excellent opportunity for choice. A playlist is a set of assignments or tasks students must complete by a given date. At the beginning of the year, I give students the same homework set (playlist). As students progress and I identify ability, I alter the playlists to accommodate the students falling out of the sleigh and those needing a faster pace. As an aside, 80% of students are best suited for the standard playlist I design per lesson, but approximately 10% of students in my demographic fall into the "go faster" group, and the other 10% fall in the "go slower" group.

A variation on playlists is to allow students to choose what is on their playlist or when they complete different items in the playlist. For example, an elementary teacher may post the playlist for the day. Students choose what and when they do something with the understanding that everything must be completed by the time the last bell rings. In another instance, a junior high teacher provides a list of six options for a weekly playlist. Students choose any 4 of the 6 options to complete by Friday at the end of class.

Playlists also provide an excellent way to add value while keeping every student occupied in a class period. All teachers experience the indifferent or highly efficient students who complete work before everyone else and are at a loss for what to do next. Playlists can fill in the gaps and still add value. Perhaps an art teacher allows students to pick three art projects as a playlist to be completed by the end of the term. It is expected that students complete their playlist over 10 weeks on their own time at home. However, when students complete in-class projects before due dates, they may work on their playlist during class. The choice in playlist design, when to complete tasks, and where they are completed all foster pull and add value to student learning.

Kanban

When allowing students to pull their education, when does a teacher or student know mastery is achieved? Traditionally, the answer from both groups is passing a test. Seasoned teachers use formative and summative assessments. All are correct. These each represent a *signal*, or evidence of mastery so the student can move to the next stage in the learning process. In Lean Think, the signal is called Kanban. The principle of Kanban is to watch for indicators that show the customer is pulling the product. Kanban gives workers new eyes to recognize indicators within a process that point to a customer pulling the product.

Look at an example from manufacturing. A worker on a manufacturing line has exactly 10 screws in a bucket. One screw is used for each product. When the bucket is empty, that signals 10 customers pulled the product. What about in a grocery store? As produce aisles and canned good shelves empty, store workers are signaled to replenish goods due to customer consumption, or pull. The food is only replaced as food is purchased. Even the classroom provides another good example: I purchase a case of tissue boxes every year. In the fall and spring, students use fewer tissues because of decreased sickness. But in winter, tissues fly out of the boxes. Every box I throw away presents the rate of pull of students consuming tissues from runny noses.

My favorite example of Kanban comes from book fairs. I adore children's books. My second daughter was a fan of the *Fancy Nancy* series. At every book fair, we were on the lookout for the high demand, brightly colored, sparkly *Fancy Nancy* covers. At one fair, I was thrilled to grab the last book on the lovely display shelf. As I passed the glittered hardback to the cashier, she removed a bookmark from the animated pages that read, "Last book in stock." She then told me she could not sell the book but had to order more. She kindly took my information, and my daughter had the treasured volume in her hands the next day. Before leaving the fair, I scanned the shelves more closely. Sure enough, the last book in each pile had the same bookmark. Very smart. As book lovers purchased books, or pulled the product, the worker's signal to reorder was a bookmark in the last available book.

Teachers routinely draft an array of signals to identify student mastery. However, do students also recognize the signals? For students to take control and pull their education, they must be trained to identify their own signals in learning, or Kanban. An obvious way to train students to recognize mastery learning is for teachers to simply share the signals they look for, like an 80% proficiency on a test, 4 on a rubric, completion of a task within in 5 minutes, or 100% accuracy. Teachers can publish mastery markers for student awareness and possession.

Several other methods help students identify Kanban. Take metacognition, or coaching young people to think about their own thinking. As pupils learn self-talk, they grow the ability to assess personal progress. When students can set goals with a distinct measure to qualify mastery, they are measuring their learning. When students clearly understand rubrics, how to fulfill requirements, and interpret scoring, then they are gauging how successful they are. Rubrics offer both quantitative and descriptive competency feedback.

Education is on the precipice of change, transitioning the long-held push system into a combination push/pull system. The competency movement is in the fledging stages as teachers experiment with standards-based grading, online instruction, flex learning, flipped classes, and synchronous/asynchronous lessons.

This powerhouse generation of educators is the one to refine and perfect transfer of control to students by modeling push yet encouraging pull. As a result, pupils focus on understanding and mastering the material instead of jumping through hoops just to get a grade. At each grade level, students increase their time on their individual sled until they sit in strong control of their education. Here are rapid-fire ideas to implement pull:

- Allow students to work ahead
- Provide students resources for extra instruction
- Create playlists
- Give students a window for completion
- Allow students to choose playlist options
- Differentiate playlists based on student need
- Give students choice in assessments or assignments
- Make minimum pace obvious and establish accountability
- Consistently uphold natural consequences as students miss due dates or lack proficiency
- Focus on understanding, not the grade
- Have students set measurable goals
- Help students identify signals that indicate mastery
- Goals
- Interpreting rubrics
- Proficiency cutoffs

Gemba Walks

Gemba means "go to the place where value is added," and the best place to add value is where the product is made. In manufacturing, managers go to the assembly line. In education, people go to the classroom (or screen) because student learning is the product. Gemba walks happen on multiple levels in education: teacher to student, teacher to teacher, administration to teacher, PLC to PLC, and school to school. Interestingly, Toyota encourages managers to spend 50% of their time "in Gemba," observing processes of product creation.

Four verbs describe what goes on in a Gemba walk: observe, engage, improve, and respect. All parties, the observer and observed, show respect to one another, have open minds for change, and remember they are on the same team. During observation, the observer focuses on processes, not people. Often, to really understand what's going on in the classroom, observers engage the observed with questions of clarification and explanation. Lastly, the observer mentally processes everything gleaned from the Gemba walk with improvement as the end goal. The observer identifies items from the experience to improve their own classroom. They also respectfully offer thoughts for improvement from what was observed.

While I observe, I ask myself: What can I learn and what can I give? Ironically, two of my most poignant Gemba walks were observing master teachers outside my content. It was magical watching an AP Art History teacher inspire his students with passion for antiquity. He gave me permission to radiate my enthusiasm for chemistry. An AP Statistics teacher eloquently modeled how to question students for high level thinking. I use her questioning techniques to this day.

Before taking Gemba walks, have a plan.

- What is the goal of the Gemba walk?
- Is there an emphasis? Does the observed want you to watch for something?
- Focus on process
- Document observations
- Ask questions
- Follow up with personal application
- Follow up with feedback to the observed

In teacher/student observations, the teacher goes to the student. Proximity is key. Directly observe what the student does in their learning process, whether it be in a classroom, lab, on a screen, or during an outdoor activity. Ask students the why, how, and what regarding their work. Again, I am constantly asking myself: What can I learn from observing their processes and how can I best support them? On a personal note, I love daily Gemba walks with my students. A closeness and connection occur as we share the learning process together. I give ample smiles and shower encouragement, offer compliments and shoot queries. Gemba walks prove a highlight of the class period for each of us.

Teacher/teacher observations are like gold. When observing other teachers, you always learn through examples and non-examples. Observe educators in your specific content/grade level and outside of your teaching expertise. Pay attention to activities, technology, transitions, and especially the customer. Where is value being added to student learning? What did you observe? Look for things to integrate into your teaching practice and identify constructive observations to share.

The highest functioning Gemba walks I have seen are from a principal at a Title I elementary school. Interestingly, this principal was the counselor at my daughters' elementary school years ago. Each of my girls adored him as he was exceptional even then. Since moving into administration, he has remade two different Title I schools. One of his key tools, Gemba walks. With psychological safety, clipboards, and the above list, teachers observe teachers to learn from and support one another. The ultimate beneficiary — the students in the teachers' classrooms.

I have observed educators teaching all levels of K-12, in subjects ranging from English to math. Gemba observations make me a better teacher. I recently advised a second-year junior high math teacher to observe a veteran math teacher to watch her grading techniques. There is no reason to reinvent the wheel, or a successful math grading system, when it already exists.

As a PLC, watch other PLC meetings and classroom instruction. For example, my school's social studies PLC launched an experimental credit recovery program. Other PLCs in the school went and observed the social studies model. Those PLCs evaluated their own credit recovery methods. Having observed the social studies trial, differing PLCs garnered new ideas and a fresh perspective to improve their programs. In fact, this year my science department is launching a new credit recovery class modeled after our social studies department's experiment. I predict it will be significantly more effective than our past science credit recovery, and we only discovered this because we "observed and engaged" another department.

When administration observes teacher classrooms, we see two advantages. First, administrators are experienced educators. A wealth of insight and knowhow reside within administrative teams. Second, administrators have a thousand-foot view of the school and district. Teachers are in the trenches and only see the whites of students' eyes. Embedded in the daily grind of education, the classroom dictates a teacher's perspective. Administrators are privileged to see a wider picture of how parts fit together. Their input is invaluable in building a class that benefits students within the context of the school's and district's larger goals.

My first-year teaching, one administrator gently observed I used the term "you guys" repeatedly. Another recommended I jot down a few amendments in a particular lab to increase efficiency the next year students performed the same lab. These observations were very helpful, and I am thankful for the time principals have spent in my room. A dear friend and principal of an elementary school always asks teachers prior to observation what they are most interested in. His tip to effectively observe teachers is to ask if there is anything specific the teacher wants the observer to watch for.

School-to-school observations are uniquely helpful. Education teams get to see different cultures, ideas, resources, and practices in action. The experience broadens the mindset of observers and engenders greater vision. The underlying purpose for all observation is improvement, so both the observer and observed must be willing to give, receive, and implement. Then, they take what is given and utilize it to improve student learning in one's sphere of influence. Observing a school outside my district birthed the radically new idea of a Para-Instructor class. Terrific value derives from observing different schools because it fosters bigger dreams.

Superimpose the idea of control onto Gemba walks. Both parties give up a degree of control. The observed are vulnerable in being watched and receiving feedback from the observers. The observers lay aside preconceived notions and view processes with an open heart to learn and grow. If both parties remain open and remember they are on the same team, then mutual respect allows for transferred and shared control.

Meetings

When asked to describe educational meetings, attendees typically groan and roll their eyes as they recount what transpired. Participants sit and listen to piles of information consuming their very precious resource of time. What is the real truth? The most valuable meeting is the meeting that never happened. Informational items should be sent in emails. This only works, however, if all participants agree to read the emails. Unread emails translate into handholding and babysitting in the form of a meeting.

Effective meetings are also a form of Gemba walks. People bring ideas, concerns, and data to devise ways to add value to student learning. In essence, individuals present their classroom Gemba walk observations to get input from others. The most productive meetings contain the following components:

- An agenda is sent to all participants prior to the meeting
- Time limit has been established
- Entire team is present (or the meeting is recorded)
- It is data driven
- The customer (students) is the focus
- The goal is the target

- The question, "Does this add value?" is center
- Constantly press for improvement based on data
- Reflect on learning lessons

Remember, control rests in the hands of the expert. Lean Think recognizes administration, teachers, parents, and students as experts in what they do. As such, each can possess and manage control through a pull system. Teachers mentor and support students by modeling educational learning through the push system. With scaffolded actions to transfer control, students gradually take ownership of learning and pull their education independently. Gemba walks are versions of sharing control between the teacher/student and professional/professional. All involved look to learn from one another while observing and sharing insights.

Mastery in student learning is the goal for every child. That is only accomplished through respect for individuals and proper placement of responsibilities. Everyone working together (with egos set aside) opens pathways for students to receive their education at an optimum rate through a positive experience. Here is a rapid-fire list for Gemba walks:

- Teachers observe students with proximity and through data
- Teachers observe teachers
- Same and different content
- Same and different grade levels
- Administrators observe teachers
- Schools observe schools
- Move information from meetings to emails
- In meetings, share observations/data from the classroom and provide discussion
- In meetings, share lessons learned from Gemba walks
- In Gemba walks, identify what can be learned from the observation and what can be shared with the observed

Chapter 18: The Scientific Process

The final Lean tool is just a version of the scientific process: Plan Do Check Adjust (PDCA). PDCA came from a Bell Telephone physicist, Walter Shewhart, in the 1930s. He is called the Father of Statistical Quality Control (Best, 2006). This is a method to try something new with a feedback loop to direct future changes. PDCA provides the vehicle to combine all tools and apply them in an efficient manner. The flow of PDCA feels intuitive and obvious, which affords easy application. Look at the outline of steps to mentally create an organization schematic.

- Plan: Identify the issue and design a plan for change
    o Use assumptions from data to drive decisions
    o Draft a minimum viable product (MVP) for implementation
- Do: Carry out the plan
    o Experiment
    o Collect data
- Check: Evaluate results
    o Engage voice of the customer (VOC)
- Adjust: Respond to data
    o Keep
    o Trash
    o Tweak
- Repeat

The PDCA cycle, when applied to education, begins when a teacher recognizes a need and responds to it. Not surprisingly, teachers execute PDCA on a microscale hundreds of times within a week. They constantly identify an issue, devise a quick plan, do it, gauge effectiveness, and make a mental note for future reference. Large-scale PDCA provides a mechanism to tackle significant improvement problems, for instance, how to remediate students with low exam performance. As a reminder, never change something simply for the sake of change. Change should only respond to a needed improvement.

Plan

Identifying a needed improvement activates the plan stage. An effective plan begins with assumptions which, in turn, lead to a Minimum Viable Product. Assumptions are the current understanding of a situation and tentative ideas about how to amend it. Perception of an issue comes from data, student input, observations, experience, and intuition. Based on everything known and using teacher expertise, assumptions shape the plan.

For example, fewer students earned proficiency on a recent test compared to years past (data). An assembly robbed review time (observation). Students complained the unit felt too fast (input). The content is more rigorous than other units (experience). The teacher hypothesizes that the lack of review made the students feel rushed and hindered academic connections solidifying learning (intuition). Based on these assumptions, the teacher makes a plan to rectify the immediate issue so they can be prepared for future situations.

Minimum Viable Product

With assumptions identified, begin drafting a planned response. Devise the smallest and simplest working model to address an issue. This is called the Minimum Viable Product (MVP) (Ries, 2011). While creating a plan, the goal is not perfection. The goal is to add value to students as quickly and effectively as possible. This means the plan does not need to be 100% polished. The issue requires a response that quickly adapts to student needs during the process. It is the idea of fixing a car while it is moving. I want to launch the smallest solution to an improvement so I do not waste time on things that will not have a positive impact. I also need flexibility to change things easily in response to feedback.

Here is a non-example of MVP and the mistakes I made several years ago. Our chemistry PLC administered a mid-year, pre-assessment test. We wanted to gauge student learning with respect to preparedness for the end-of-year final. Were the students on track to successfully take the final exam in four months? Approximately 15% of students scored below our mid-year benchmark. So, we brainstormed a plan to intercept these students before it was too late for remediation. Our solution was targeted remediation by content standard. I collected specific review questions for each standard, made purple cardstock covers, added a polyvinyl protector sheet, and personally bound 30 review books. Each teacher emailed parents a student invitation to attend focused reviews during lunch or after school. Teachers pulled aside the struggling students and asked they attend reviews on the areas where they scored below proficiency on core concepts. Each teacher took a standard to host review. The entire month of February was organized and calendared for the honors and general chemistry remediation.

Of the 15% (approximately 75 students) needing remediation, about two students showed up for each review. It was one of the biggest fails ever. The books looked fantastic, and the robust review calendar impressed coworkers, but unfortunately, all those efforts added no value to students. The piece we overlooked, the demographic scoring below proficiency, is not the demographic that frequents school outside of classroom time. An MVP approach would have been to copy review questions for one standard and invite students to attend 1 of 3 identical reviews within a five-day period. Had we used the MVP model, our time and effort would have been saved and redirected toward something truly valuable.

Now look at a positive example utilizing an MVP. Four years ago, my administration informed the faculty that our websites would no longer be supported. Everything was moving to Canvas, a Learning Management System (LMS). I had limited experience with Canvas, so I was slightly panicked. I needed student help to shape my approach while designing my Canvas courses. Thankfully, our English and math departments had already been using Canvas, so the students had exposure and knowhow with the LMS. Their experience would help me form assumptions to then shape new Canvas courses.

I gave the students a two-question survey at the end of the school year. As free response questions, I simply asked what they liked and disliked about Canvas. The data from the "dislike" question: Students despised typing answers into Canvas, and they did not like learning from tools posted on the LMS. The data from the "like" question: They really liked immediate feedback from inputting homework answers to see if they were correct, and they valued all the learning tools available online when they were absent. I read the data, baffled, and thought, do they not see the obvious correlations? The only way to receive immediate feedback on work is to input it into Canvas. They were making it hard for me! Yet, from the seemingly conflicting responses, I came up with some working assumptions:

- Students value available online learning resources when they are absent.
- When in class, students favor direct instruction and interaction with the teacher, not online learning tools.
- Students prefer to do homework with pencil and paper.
- Students desire real time feedback while completing homework at home to ensure accuracy and understanding.

With those assumptions, again, thanks to input from students, I designed a Minimum Viable Product. The July before school began, I designed one term, 10 weeks, for the two courses I was going to teach. I uploaded all the online resources I had collected throughout the years so students had everything they needed to continue learning if they were absent. Additionally, for each homework assignment, I posted randomized odd answers. Students could then do their homework at home and check to see if their odd answers were somewhere on the list of correct answers. This provided enough feedback to confirm they were on the right track without making them input answers. It also kept them accountable and honest to do their own work.

At the beginning of the school year, I told the students my Canvas courses were an experiment and asked that they please make mental notes of how to improve them. At seven weeks, I surveyed the students and asked one question: What would they change to make the course better and more user-friendly? I received over 500 ideas. Many were repeats or versions of the same idea, but I was amazed by the responses! With outstanding feedback, I designed the rest of the school year, making 20 significant changes to the original construction. Every change represented an insightful idea from a student.

Had I followed the traditional tactic of trying to make everything perfect and complete, I would have 1 of 2 wastes: either the students would have wasted time on a subpar course, confused for an entire year, or I would have wasted huge amounts of time reworking and fixing defects throughout the year. By launching the smallest working product possible, I received early feedback to add more value to students sooner. It saved me time, too: I created the remaining terms with one touch the right way, the first time, and I had no reworks.

Note the steps working with an MVP. First, I solicited student input. Next, based on customer feedback, I consciously identified my assumptions and clarified the approach for the task. From assumptions, I designed the simplest functioning product possible. I told the students the product was an experiment and asked them to make observations throughout its use. This brought students into the improvement cycle. Then I collected data early in the process and immediately made changes. What was the driving force in this process? The voice of my customer reflected in data to identify what added the most value. The flexibility of the MVP allowed me to instantly respond, tweak, and increase value. The most powerful advantage afforded by the MVP is the agility to immediately adjust practices and dial in the value without wasted time or resources. Here is the process again:

- Form assumptions based on data, observation, and expertise
- Draft Minimum Viable Product: smallest, simplest, most flexible solution
- Collect MVP responses early in implementation
- Immediately respond to input and make changes

Voice of the Customer (VOC)

Throughout the book, I have shared examples where I solicit student feedback. This feedback is called the Voice of the Customer (VOC). Listening to the VOC means understanding the collective needs, wants, and dreams of those receiving a product. For example, a car manufacturer is only going to make a car the customer is willing to buy. The company does research and polls present and future customers as to which amenities they want on a car. If prospective purchasers want cars with sunroofs, engineers design a sunroof. If customers do not want leather seats, the manufacturer will not waste resources installing leather seats.

For a student to get exactly what they need, want, and desire, communication must be synchronized between the teacher and student. The teacher only knows what the student needs if the student tells them, and the student only tells them if they are asked. Therefore, an organized, purposeful feedback loop from student to teacher must be established so both parties can be on the same page.

In education, the teacher receives feedback from students. However, because students are minors, teachers must help students identify their needs, wants, and desires. The real benefit of student feedback is fine-tuning the logistics in teaching practices. As mentioned earlier, I tell students I am the expert at teaching, and they are the experts at learning. I do not sit in their seats every day or have the same view of the classroom. I do not touch the LMS page daily to access homework or resources. I do not collaborate in lab groups doing experiments. Collecting data from various measures provides a partial picture of classroom effectiveness, but the students' perspectives give the needed, final insight on practical usage of tools and activities. Their feedback is necessary to fully answer the question, "Does this add value?"

Maybe not surprisingly, the best ideas I have implemented in my classroom have come from students. The VOC proves one of the greatest resources in a teacher's arsenal of tools. Students have shown me details I would never notice or consider without their feedback. A few student ideas I implemented after the Canvas MVP survey included breaking the calendar into months rather than a term, highlighting each unit in a different color, and adding the eBook link to the front page.

My favorite student idea was highlighting the homework assignment on each agenda. Several students, with honesty and transparency, shared they did not care or read anything on the daily agenda except for the assignment. They asked if I would please highlight the homework so they could quickly identify assigned problems without searching the entire agenda. That was no problem; it takes me two seconds to highlight homework in neon yellow when I type the agenda. It saves each student that much time by not sifting through agenda information. Absent students still have all the information they need from the agenda, and everyone else gets precisely what they want by reading the yellow line of homework. This two-way communication, feedback loop from student to teacher, becomes part of the classroom process. Teachers design activities with student input in mind. Student needs, wants, and desires form assumptions which then drive MVP creation. As the MVP is implemented, teachers receive student feedback, which repeats the process. Teachers respond with improvements and the cycle continues.

An impressive byproduct of seeking student feedback is students take ownership of their learning. The classroom culture shifts from "us against them" to "we are a team." Respect and appreciation for student ideas affirm their crucial position in the learning process. Students must be engaged and active in their learning. When they are asked how to do things better and are allowed to submit thoughts and ideas, students openly see the importance of their dynamic participation. Requesting student feedback provides affirmation of their worth and influence in their own education. They are more willingly take the academic reins in a cultural setting where their personal experience is valued and directs decisions in the classroom.

Solicit student feedback both formally and informally. It just depends on the extent of feedback desired and how fast you need it. For end-of-year, end-of-term, or large project feedback, I issue surveys. A word of warning: Give the fewest questions possible and tell students how long the survey will take, e.g., three questions and two minutes. My go-to questions are:

- What helped you the most … (This identifies what to keep)
- What was not useful … (This shows what to get rid of)
- If you were the teacher, what would you change … (This is the most useful question!)

I ask students to please be kind. They are evaluating the class and not me as a person. I also remind myself they are young and not to take things personally. A thicker skin helps when reading some of the comments. If needed, share responses with a coworker to get another perspective on interpreting student answers. Overall, it's best to provide anonymous surveys, but when using my LMS, the survey responses are tied to a student account. Students may not feel as comfortable being honest about ideas if they don't like something we do; they do not want to hurt our feelings. So, try using one of several free survey tools for anonymous feedback.

I frequently do informal surveys. At the end of an activity, for example, I may quickly poll students for effectiveness. How useful was this? Did this activity clearly illustrate XYZ? I ask everyone to raise their hand with an assessment of 1-5 fingers. Five is highly valuable and one is not valuable. Then I field a few questions from each side of the spectrum probing for the "why" using finger assessment. I make mental notes about what to change for the next class or write thoughts in my lecture notes for next year. Informal feedback works at the end of a unit, quiz, activity, lecture, resource application, or discussion.

The plan section of PDCA sets the stage for every organized improvement. It is worth the time to look at data, both observational and numeric, to direct planning. From data, develop assumptions to lay the groundwork shaping the plan. Consider the Voice of the Customer and constantly ask, "Does this add value?" All the while, keep the goal and measure in front of the entire process. You will ultimately create stellar plans that require minimal rework or tweaking. The physicist Shewhart had no idea his PDCA methodology would one day take root in every facet of life, even education.

Chapter 19: The Feedback Loop

Plan in PDCA establishes the foundation upon which to build improvements. Once in a Lean Think workshop, a shop teacher shared that he used to build houses prior to entering education. On his first job, the foreman carefully measured and aligned everything on the site for an exact foundation. The teacher said he was a bit perturbed because all the workers were wasting time waiting for the foreman, who appeared to be in no rush as he meticulously prepped the site. The teacher later realized the value of laying a precise foundation when he began setting logs for the cabin. He said they came together flawlessly and speedily. The time invested to prepare a solid foundation was returned many times over once building began. Likewise, with a solid educational plan in place, effective building occurs in the classroom.

Do: The Real Work Begins

Doing can be daunting. Fear of failing or anxiety about wasting effort keeps teachers from trying something new. I use a different word — EXPERIMENT! I love experiments. Here is a truth: Experiments never fail because you always learn something. In an experiment, the point is to evaluate data from a procedure to gain knowledge and shape future steps. That happens in any experiment, inside or outside a lab. Using the word "experiment" removes the pressure to be perfect. It also lessens anxiety about trying something new and different. Experiments appear more flexible than concrete. They afford an opportunity to *try* something rather than *commit* to something.

It is much less overwhelming to experiment with a new grading scale for a year than to implement a new grading scale. In both situations, the new grading scale applies to student performance, but at the end of the year, it is mentally easier to amend the grading scale when it was only an *experiment*. In department or PLC meetings, when someone presents an idea and it receives positive discussion, I say, "Let's do an experiment." We go through assumptions, craft an MVP, and then execute the ... experiment. With groups, I find a greater willingness to attempt new things, look for incremental improvement, and change broken processes when calling it an experiment.

In 1519, when Hernan Cortes landed in California, he burned 10 of his 11 ships, removing any hope of going home the way his 600 men had come (Smith, 2019). They were all in, whether or not they wanted to be. Well, teachers do not need to feel the same permanency when making changes in the classroom. Teachers can be leery of change because they think they are burning all their ships. Instead, approach the "do" in PDCA with an experimental attitude. While doing the experiment, collect data and keep the customer and goal in focus. Consistently ask, "Does this add value?" Then, with peace and confidence, adjust to continually increase value. Teachers merely try something new to see if it works better. If not, then do another experiment!

Check

Check in PDCA is the same as the measure in Chapter 2. Data drives Lean Think. Classroom decisions derive from qualitative (observational) and quantitative (numeric) data. Data reveals if the implemented plan improved student learning. It further narrows the path to achieve optimum student learning by zeroing in on greatest value. This is commonly the step where classrooms drop the ball. Teachers present innovative ideas and invest energy to create new resources based on those ideas, but then they do not check if the changes produced the intended outcome. The check step is the feedback loop by which future decisions are made. Changes only have prime impact if there is follow-up with data analysis. According to data, did the change improve student learning?

Two additional tools help assess effectiveness of experiments: cohort and split tests. A cohort test uses the same group and changes conditions in trials. A split test is two groups with identical conditions with one variable between the groups.

I ran a cohort test to identify the best way to utilize virtual labs. The cohort comprised all my honors chemistry students and tested different methods of administering virtual labs. The measures were post-lab questions and unit exams. In one term, all students completed four virtual labs. Virtual Lab 1 was one of three rotations performed in one day: physical, informational, and virtual rotations. Virtual Lab 2 was in conjunction with a physical lab on a lab day. The students had 90 minutes to complete both the physical and virtual labs in any order they chose. Virtual Lab 3 was given as an at-home introduction to be completed before Unit 3 began. Virtual Lab 4 replaced the physical lab for Unit 4. Every class did all four virtual labs the same way. Comparing lab and exam scores to past years, what conclusion did I draw? None of the virtual lab applications significantly improved student learning. Physical labs far exceed virtual labs in understanding and skill acquisition. I now only use virtual labs for absences. Students must complete two virtual labs for every one physical lab missed, and they may only do this once a term.

The second assessment tool is split tests, or two different groups doing identical things with one difference. My wonderful colleague, also teaching honors chemistry next door to my room, ran a "retake" split test. This was our toes dipping in the water of standards-based grading. We did everything identical between our honors chemistry classes: same pace, labs, demos, assignments, and tests. The one difference was she allowed unlimited retakes on tests, and I did not. We compared unit tests and the term final exam.

The results were a wash. Students who retook unit tests did not perform any better on the final exam. The data did not persuade us that simply allowing students to retake a test increased learning. Observationally, my counterpart noticed students opting to retake tests were more concerned about their grades than gaining knowledge. Using that data as the feedback, she implemented PDCA again. In the second iteration, she tweaked requirements. Students must follow a set of remediations before allowed to retake a test. The jury is still out on effectiveness as we continue to collect and compare data.

Notice the model in both assessments. Assumptions, based on data and experience, inspire a plan. While implementing the plan, data is collected and evaluated. Feedback from data informs future changes (assumptions) to begin a new plan, and the cycle continues.

Adjust

Adjust responds to the data (Check), both qualitative and quantitative. Much of a teacher's evaluation comes from observation. Teachers, being experts in both education and children, pick up on fine nuances to refine the effectiveness of their practices. Do not discount the value and power of observation — or a gut feeling. Albeit, nothing speaks louder than numbers. Dig into numbers and let them honestly speak. Looking at data is not intended to shame or degrade a teacher's effort. The purpose of data is to enlighten areas and ways to adjust. Data points the direction for improvement.

When reflecting upon data, ask the question: "What can I learn from this?" Identify 1-3 main takeaways from the experiment. With those in mind, the next mental step determines *how* to adjust. There are three choices for adjust: keep, trash, or tweak.

If on the first try, your choice is to keep whatever you experimented with, then you've experienced the rare, yet magical, instance when everything in the plan worked and student learning increased better than expected. Do not touch it! It is perfect just the way it is. This is like getting a child ready for school pictures. They look angelic walking out the door. The hope is they makes it through recess and lunch without mud, scrapes, or tussled hair before it is finally their turn to sit for the photograph. I would tell my girls, "You can breathe between now and picture time, but that is about it. Please try and stay perfect before pictures! Then you can play hard."

One of my best classroom keep moments was instituting "Life Lessons with Laub." Right before I go through the agenda at the beginning of the class period, I share a life lesson. I got the idea from Ron Clark's, *The Essential 55*. I explicitly teach my daughters life lessons, so why not my students? Students love it and the lessons become a nice relationship building tool. I ask them to consider scenarios like this: "If you have an involved question for a teacher, and the person standing behind you only needs to hand the teacher a paper, let them go before you. The same is true for grocery stores. If your basket is full of groceries and the person behind you holds two items, let them go ahead of you." As an experiment, I instituted the Life Lessons and learned I did not need to change anything to achieve better than desired impact. I kept the experiment as is. This is unusual and has happened maybe twice in my teaching career. In contrast, many times I go through several iterations of an improvement and eventually achieve a "keep" status. It happens very rarely the first time around.

The second choice, trash, is also atypical. Very few things teachers try are such a failure that the best thing to do is light it on fire, walk away, and never look back. Unfortunately, I have had more "trash" experiences than "keep" victories. Five years into teaching AP chemistry, I had a great idea, or so I thought. Every April, the second Saturday before the AP exam, students take a full 3.5-hour practice exam. This particular year, I decided to make it even more meaningful for students. I determined to cook them all breakfast in my classroom before the test. It would be a mini celebration of their hard work and ensure they had food in their stomachs before the practice test. I discovered not even food is good enough compensation to get students out of bed at 7:30 on a Saturday morning. Let me just say, it was a huge amount of work to cook for 60 students, and they were not overly enthused by the early morning meal. It was the first and LAST time I cooked breakfast for all my students on a weekend.

Experiments you keep or trash become obvious very quickly. But the third choice, tweak, represents the majority of the PDCA adjust. Because assumptions are driven by data, thus directing the plan, classroom experiments frequently come close to hitting the mark. They just need fine tuning to polish the process. The fine tuning happens by engaging PDCA ... again. Using data from the check step, form new assumptions, draft a revised plan, do it, and collect data along the way. For the classroom setting, the second go-around usually achieves the goal with the level of desired quality. For larger projects, three or more iterations may be required to sharpen a process. Keep using the PDCA loop while integrating all the great lessons from Lean Think. Here are rapid-fire ideas where to implement PDCA:

- Every process improvement (Yes, this encompasses them all!)

Respect

Respect for every person in the organization — student, teacher, and administration — is crucial in PDCA. Mutual respect recognizes each person is the expert in the part they play in the learning process. The individual possesses unique experiences, knowledge, gifts, talents, and abilities.

Through the power of respect, individuals are emboldened to take ownership of their position in the learning process. They share ideas, generate experiments, and actively move learning forward.

The culture melds into a team mindset of, "We work together to produce the best student learning possible." Everyone rises to their potential by fully utilizing talents. Through respect, people feel valued, morale increases, the culture is healthy, and ultimately, student learning improves.

I shared this principle with the Utah State Board of Education Teaching and Learning Directors at a Lean Think workshop. One director raised his hand and commented that some education leaders see such incompetence in a percentage of teachers that they feel compelled to create regulations to force minimum teaching compliance. Regrettably, a handful of professionals at every school should not be in education. It is not for lack of ability; it is for lack of effort and commitment. No amount of respect or authority motivates them to any degree of excellence. An answer to this issue is accountability.

It goes back to defining facets of the classroom: customer, goal, and measure. Who is the customer, what is the goal, and how is the goal measured? These tenets must be clear, communicated, agreed upon, and repeated. Individuals are then expected to work toward the highest levels of quality through incremental process improvement. Data gauges improvement and discussion ensues. Educators purposefully work to add value, and they make progress and confirm it through assessment. Teachers who struggle, but genuinely care and willingly try, can be mentored into outstanding educators. Measures hold every person in the educational system accountable to work toward the goal and refine practices to accomplish the goal.

The concern is educators who do not work for the benefit of students. Rules will not bring success into their rooms. The extra regulations just stifle educators who are doing great things with students. The indifferent educator or administrator must be addressed by administrative/district warning protocols and subsequent consequences.

194

Summary

Plan Do Check Adjust is the vehicle to apply all other Lean Think tools and waste removal. It provides a practical, workable model to implement incremental process improvement. Encompassing every facet of education is respect. Success only happens in the classroom when every individual at every level feels respected. Regardless of position, a person is valued for who they are. Additionally, each job is valued. No one is labeled as mere "labor" and no task is identified as inferior. Each person is the expert at the position they hold, and each position positively adds to student learning experiences. Establishing respect and a solid plan is like establishing the foundation of a strong building. As the do, check, and adjust steps transpire, the rest of the building smoothly comes together. Ultimately, moving through the mechanism of PDCA, with respect and kindness, makes the way for a successful educational enterprise.

PART IV: Summary

Chapter 20: Pulling It All Together

At times in my classroom, I see students get lost in the trees. They can no longer differentiate the forest from the encroaching foliage. They miss the main point of my lesson because they are entrenched in the details. This happens with significant figures, a scientific practice of only writing numbers that represent a real value. Students become so concerned with writing the accurate number of significant figures that they forget to focus on the content at hand. I verbally warn students about the pitfall and give permission to look up and see the forest. I tell them to focus on specific heat in theory and math application, for instance, and just do their best on significant figures. We have all year to perfect writing digits. Do not emphasize them now, and instead, concentrate on the present, important topic.

I share the same analogy with teachers. Do not get lost in the minutiae of details; focus on the big picture. The driving tenet of Lean Think is to remove waste and only do what adds value. Keep your eyes fixed on this principle. Numerous and excellent tools, ideologies, tips, tricks, and hacks are available through Lean Think, but do not let the volume of tools become overwhelming. Remember incremental process improvement. A teacher takes one step at a time to remove waste in a process and sharpen it.

It is like another favorite idiom from my grandma: You eat an elephant one bite at a time. I remember talking to her on the phone when my five daughters were under the age of six. I felt like I was failing as a mother. She would ask, "Did everyone get their diapers changed today? Did everyone get fed and bathed? Did everyone get kissed today?" I would reply yes to each question. Then she would emphatically reply, "Then you have done a good job! Remind me, how do you eat an elephant?" And I felt better. The attraction of Lean Think is that a teacher takes only one step at a time, which is consistent as a life approach, too. By centering on what adds value and identifying one task to improve right now, teachers can steadily make significant gains over time, which translates into students making significant gains.

For teachers just beginning Lean Think, the first step is waste removal. Do not worry about anything else. With passion and purpose, find waste and get rid of it. Recall my chemistry PLC only focused on waste removal for an entire year — and our students did substantially better! Focus, focus, focus on removing waste. Only keep what adds value. If new resources must be made, use Lean Think tools to design a product free of waste. Otherwise, let the mantra of waste removal be the most important guiding principle. Once waste is removed, space and time become available for sharpening valuable practices. This is where Lean Think tools come into play; improvements make already effective practices even better.

Overview

Lean Think is not a "one and done" or "check it off the list" transformation you can complete in 6-12 months. Lean Think is a culture and methodology to move through life, especially teaching. No one ever arrives at the ideal state because no one is perfect, but Lean Think helps you move closer incrementally. It takes time, and teachers must grant themselves the liberty to take enough time to sort through those things leading to improvement. Review the fundamental process for improvement:

LEAN BABY STEPS

- Define: Customer, Goal, and Measure
- Identify: Current and Future states
- Get Organized: 6S
- Kaizen: Incremental process improvement
  - Remove Waste
  - Apply Lean Tools
- Plan, Do, Check, Adjust

Remember to define the classroom by articulating the customer (always the student in education), overarching goal, and ultimate measure. Next, identify current and ideal states of the classroom. Honestly examine what you see in the classroom, and what student performance is like at present. Then ponder and imagine what an ideal setting and student performance within that setting look like. With classroom parameters set, you can get organized with 6S: sort, straighten, scrub, systemize, standardize, and ensure safety. Finally, with parameters and organization established, a teacher can promptly begin improvement.

Kaizen is the mindset of incremental process improvement. It is taking one bite of the elephant at a time. Improvement happens two ways: waste removal and utilizing Lean Think tools. As mentioned before, always start with waste removal. Probe for the presence of the nine wastes found in education:

- Movement
- Time
- Overproduction
- Knowledge
- Talent
- Capacity
- Process and Handling
- Assets
- Defects

It may take time removing waste, but that is all right. By doing less (removing waste), education becomes more focused on valuable procedures. Student learning improves and teachers regain time in their personal lives. Once waste is eradicated, then tools, listed below, are implemented to polish value-adding practices. They assist teachers in creating powerful and impactful learning experiences.

- Load Leveling
- Standardization
- Flow
- Andon Cord
- Just in Time
- Error Proofing
- Jidoka
- Push vs. Pull
- Kanban
- Gemba Walks
- PDCA
- Minimum Viable Product
- Voice of the Customer
- Respect

After a while, integrating tools and continually watching for waste becomes a lifestyle. One step at a time, one improvement at a time, the teacher reshapes their classroom, making it better every year. The process is manageable because the teacher works on one specific need at a time. Once that need is met, the process begins again with the next most important task or need.

The teacher uses assumptions to plan a course removing waste and/or sharpening tools. They execute the plan, then check the data to evaluate feedback. Driven by the data, amendments are made, and a new loop begins. Educators are amazed at the incredible progress students make by consistently using Lean Think as the classroom improvement mechanism. The icing on the cake? Teachers increase their job satisfaction, and it takes less time to produce a stellar product. Teachers go home earlier!

Actionable Items: Priorities

This is where the rubber meets the road. Where and how to begin are paramount questions. There are several ways to launch Lean Think in a classroom. For a new teacher or a teacher designing a new course, the good news is you have no waste! The key for a teacher in this position is to keep the waste out. Begin with load leveling the entire year, then unit, and finally each day. At every point possible, standardize practices, which means to do those repetitive tasks the same way every time. Next, pick two tools to emphasize in resource creation. Because there are so many tools to choose from, it takes time to become an expert at implementing each of them. Experiment! But eventually, each tool becomes the automatic approach in any designing process. Until you get to that point, focus on using two tools at a time until they emerge like second nature. Once those two tools are mastered, adopt two more tools for emphasis in planning processes. All the while, guard against waste. The greatest weapon against waste is asking the question, "Does this add value?" Frame the question with the backdrop of the goal and measure(s). Using these initial steps, new teachers and new courses are well on their way to facilitating successful student learning with optimum efficiency.

For most teachers, practices and resources are already established. The task is to improve existing habits without feeling overwhelmed. The best place to start is by removing waste! Set the customer, goal, and measure squarely in front of every decision. Apply the filter to everything used or done, asking, "Does this add value?" Remember the quick win ideology: Remove the most accessible wastes first. Then look to the most impactful wastes and take the time to eradicate them. Prioritize the order in which wastes are removed. To develop expertise in waste, categorize waste as it is removed. For example, note that an assignment is removed because it is a *waste of talent* or a supply box is moved because its placement *wasted motion and time*. The ability to label waste helps prevent future waste.

It may new resources must be made to eliminate waste. Maintain waste removal as the long-term focus, but take necessary time to create new resources using Lean Think tools so you don't embed new waste. Do it right the first time and add the amount of quality appropriate for the task.

In due course, seasoned Lean Think teachers simultaneously juggle waste removal and Lean Think tool implementation. They are always watching for waste to remove, employing Lean Think tools in every new resource and activity, and choosing two macro-goals a year for improvement. Next year, my two big Lean Think projects are to first, type my AP lecture notes so students have access to them when they are absent or they can use them as study guides. Second, I'm going to redo CE chemistry review assignments for more effective reviews and better unit test scores. I still constantly look for improvement on large and small scales.

Some teachers may be enthusiastic to integrate Lean Think into an individual classroom, but how can one get an entire team onboard, like a PLC, department, school, or district, to adopt Lean Think practices? I have two words: education and data. Document and then share positive changes made within a classroom using Lean Think techniques. This informs and educates colleagues. Follow the information with data. Data speaks loudly. When students begin performing better and/or teachers are spending less time, others notice. Success is attractive and enlists followers. Personally model "doing less and getting more" by focusing on what adds value. Upon seeing this kind of proof, people will gladly join the team. Of course, blitz events like Lean Think professional development workshops, books, and videos are also instrumental teaching tools to attract support. Share strengths of Lean Think you've experienced to persuade coworkers to embrace a "less is more" approach.

Strengths of Lean

The Canadian clinical psychologist, Jordan Peterson, tells people to, "Choose your sacrifice" (2020). Ultimately, every scenario in life has difficulty. There is no easy way around, under, or over life's challenges. Everything we do and experience requires some degree of work or effort. Consider these examples: It is hard to go to the gym; likewise, it is hard to be out of shape. It is hard to go to work, but it is hard not to have money. It is hard to do homework, yet it's hard (and disappointing) to fail a class and take credit recovery. Peterson says to choose your sacrifice. One way or another, challenges will come. Which one do you want?

Notice that one side of each scenario is proactive. The individual controls the decision to sacrifice now and experience gratification later. The counter decision usually provides immediate reward with disproportional challenges down the road. A seventh-grade science teacher recently told me it was work getting rid of waste and standardizing a course between himself and another teacher. I agreed and inquired about the alternative. Obviously, doing nothing would be easier right now. However, student performance would suffer next year, and strife would cloud the coworkers' interactions. Applying Lean Think now, although hard, will make for a better working relationship and improved student experience next year. Paying the price of energy and hard work early in a situation makes for a better outcome in the future.

Lean Think is work, no doubt about it. But it pays big dividends. Choosing the hard thing at the right time, implementing Lean Think in a classroom today, saves hours of work in the future while increasing student learning along the way. It produces a better product that can be repeated year after year, reaping recurring rewards. Lean Think offers tremendous benefits to both teacher and student. It does, however, have a price. I guarantee the investment will pay off many times over in the future. Choose your sacrifice when contemplating the energy, effort, and time required to improve classroom processes. You will expend the same energy now or later, with or without Lean Think. Which is better for you and students? Be encouraged by reminding yourself about Lean Think strengths, including:

- Everything is a process, so Lean is applicable in any situation
- Lean Think provides a common language and approach within education
- Encourages teacher and student engagement
- Individuals are respected as people and as experts (teacher and student)
- Emphasizes the process is as important as the product
- Adaptable in any situation
- Allows for creativity and innovation
- Removes waste
- Focuses on value
- Liberty to make changes
- Teachers give away less personal time as unpaid work
- Affords opportunity for teachers to be the best they can be
- Offers students an optimum learning experience
- Allows teachers to get back to the reason they got into education: to teach, grow, and love students

If I have learned anything about educators in the last decade, it is they are amazing people. Teachers are the most brilliant, self-sacrificing, pleasant, positive, hopeful, hardworking humans on the planet. Who can corral 30 small 6-year-olds into a sitting position, not touching anyone else, and explain how to write complete sentences? Who can tame a room full of hormonally unstable 13-year-olds and stretch them to design unique scientific experiments? Who can inspire cool and indifferent 17-year-olds to love and appreciate the sculpture *Winged Victory of Samothrace*, da Vinci's *Last Supper*, or Monet's *Sainte-Lazare Station*? Only a teacher. Skill and persuasion, firmness and care, laughter and seriousness all flow out of one capable and intelligent being — a teacher.

Despite increased classroom challenges in recent years, teachers continue to positively impact one child at a time. The true beauty behind teachers' actions is care and concern for a single child. Their desire to see an individual succeed, thrive, walk in confidence, academically grow, become equipped, and stand strong motivates them to give of themselves unlike professionals in any other occupation. Now multiply that by 30 or 200 students every year. Teachers are unstoppable in their passion for young people to reach their potential, be affirmed, and develop their gifts. We owe a debt of gratitude to every educator standing daily in front of wide eyes, fidgety extremities, and moldable minds.

Now, give those exceptional people the right tools, and an army will rise to change the world. They can turn around the lives of students consigned to difficult schools and difficult futures. The lowest academic demographics will start to rival the long-held, high ranking echelons. Frustrated educators will be liberated to explore, experiment, and pull students to success. Departments entrenched and embittered by policy and antiquated practices will become part of a team to support and boost all cohorts to greater heights. The vehicle to revolutionize the face of education is Lean Think. It not only stocks teachers' toolbelts with highly effective techniques, but it also provides the mindset and culture for success. Teachers are empowered to use their ingenuity, freed to experiment, and granted permission to take ownership of their classroom and student learning. Lean Think trims the fat of waste and pulls energy, effort, and resources into laser focus for productive student growth. Teachers' skills are optimized while student progress thrives.

I never pictured myself a teacher. Yet, it is one of the best decisions I ever made. With gratitude, I often think of my mom and dad's gracious offer to pay for my Master of Arts degree in teaching. It changed the trajectory of not only my life but also the lives of my husband, children, and students. I am so proud and honored to be named among the ranks of such a noble profession. Bringing Lean Manufacturing from industry into the education world has been an adventure. Some of the biggest learning curves, most significant challenges, and greatest rewards are a result of Lean in education. The marriage between the two entities has proven extremely fruitful. Let me be the voice to cheer on teachers in a quest for incremental process improvement. You can do this! Take the tools and keep at it. You are making a difference. Do not give up. Focus on what adds value. Remember … do less and get more. **Lean Think**!

Epilogue

Periodically teachers will ask me to share my teaching philosophy. My motto is "I love who I teach and what I teach," but my philosophy took years to develop with the help of colleagues. Early in my career, I tenaciously sought out master teachers and administrators. I watched their instruction, then peppered them with questions. I inquired about each of their teaching philosophies, and common threads emerged: knowledge and passion for content, love for students, and an exceptional ability to communicate. As I pondered what I saw, heard, and personally experienced in the classroom, themes developed. Sharing my thoughts with my husband, he came up with an excellent analogy to visually express my philosophy: a three-legged stool.

The stool seat represents effective, masterful teaching. The three legs supporting teaching practices are:

- Love for Students
- Content Expertise and Passion
- Effective Communication Skills

All three must be present for success in the classroom. If one leg is missing, the stool falls. Unfortunately, every person moving through the education system has experienced an educator missing one of the stool legs. Maybe a teacher truly cares about students and is knowledgeable in content but lacks an effective ability to communicate concepts. Or another teacher can enthusiastically engage students with verbal skill and genuine care but is devoid of content understanding. The last model is the saddest of all, the teacher who is solid in content and communicates well but is indifferent or harsh toward students. All three legs must be securely in place for a teacher to be successful. I sincerely believe content knowledge/interest and communication skills can be taught to a teacher if they lack in any way, but a love for students is either present in the heart of an educator or not. If someone does not love young people, they should not be in education.

Master teachers reinforce the strength of the legs with crossbars. The difference between a good teacher and a great teacher is the detail in supporting the three tenets of communication, content, and care for students. Imagine three supporting crossbars on the stool, each bar connecting two legs for added strength.

Between the legs of content knowledge/passion and a love for students is the ability to *grow* the student as a person by teaching life skills, building character, and equipping them with problems solving skills. Between the love for students and effective communication legs is *relationship*, which means knowing students' names and interests, and finding ways to show care and encouragement for each student. At moments, that can mean acting as part entertainer to connect with kids in the quirky, cute ways they can relate to. Then the final crossbar between content knowledge/passion and effective communication is *organization*. A teacher can only reach greatness through consistent preparation and having things readily available to students. Organization can limit or bolster teaching abilities.

The events in a classroom perform an amazing feat of not only educating young people but also helping them grow into respectable adults. Teachers do so much more than teach. When students are 25 years old and look back on their K-12 education, what will they remember and whom will they cite as favorite teachers? Collectively, all teachers prepared them for the rigors of post-secondary training/school and for life, but they won't remember much of the specific content from individual classes.

What students will recall is the love, warmth, and care of people who poured their gifts and talents into others. The list of favorite teachers who positively impacted students' lives will be those who had all three stool legs supported in the classroom: love for students, content expertise and passion, and effective communication.

Acknowledgments

So many people helped me develop Lean Think. Many thanks to the wonderful chemistry team at Davis High School as we implemented Lean Think together: Karen Ray, Keith Williams, and Frank Stevens (retired). My dear friends and Lean Think supporters within the walls of Davis High School, either practiced the principles or supported my efforts: Mylei Zachman, Jen Harward, Holly Hoyt, Natalie Leavitt, Kayla Anderson, Alli Copier, Troy Lund, Timothy Larsen, Jeff Williams, Brad Chapple, and Ross Harris. Each of my head principals in the last decade played crucial roles in my Lean Think process: Suzi Jensen and Dee Burton, thank you for taking a risk and hiring a middle-aged, inexperienced, chemist/stay-at-home mom. Richard Swanson, thank you for hosting the first Lean education conference I attended and supporting my Green Belt endeavors. Dr. Greg Wilkey, thank you for your positivity and encouragement while I juggled classroom teaching and Lean Think coaching.

People outside my school have made indelible impact on my Lean Think journey. From Davis School District, Tyson Grover, thank you for providing my first opportunity to teach a Lean Think workshop. Belinda Kuck, thank you for your unstoppable enthusiasm and for opening doors I could not open alone. Rachel Alberts, Jake Heidrich, Robert Kinghorn, and Kurt Farnsworth, thank you for your step of faith in allowing me to work with entire faculties for the first time. Stacey Howell, my first mentor and teacher friend, thank you for your openness and support. Dr. Charles Atwood, my friend and mentor from the University of

Utah, thank you for sharing your lab experience and chemical education data.

Outside my education circles, Betty and Joe Ziskovsky, thank you for writing *Optimizing Student Learning*. It was my first resource. Linda Lawliss, my amazing editor, thank you for your countless hours and for polishing the book so beautifully. Patrick Phillips, thank you for teaching the first Lean education workshop I attended. It began a purposeful journey to design Lean Think. Pastor Ron Keller, thank you for your interest in implementing Lean Think in church administration and curriculum design and for your practical help with workshop presentation aesthetics.

For those closest to me, my dear students, we conducted fabulous education experiments and continue to traverse classroom improvement together. Thank you for everything you have taught me. I love each of you and pray for your daily success despite time and distance. Shane and Kazuna Stilson, Mike and Elisa Magagna, and Stephanie Sefcik, thank you for your support and reflection during this process. I love all of you. Bob and Vicki Owen and Richard Laub, thank you for your fervent and very biased support of all I do. I love each of you. To my parents, Philip and Ruby Stilson, your unwavering love, godly examples, and unmatchable work ethics have made all the difference in my life. Thank you. Thank you also for sending me to school to become a teacher. I love you. To my five beautiful, intelligent, hardworking, smiley, and delightful daughters: Abigail, Rachel, Ariel, Ivie, and Micah, you are the joy of my heart. You will always be my baby girls. I am so proud of you. Thank you for walking, and at times enduring, this journey with me. I love you.

My precious Gregg, you had no idea what you were getting into when you got down on one knee. Thank you for teaching me Lean Manufacturing and helping me create Lean Think. Thank you for being present every step of the journey. Your insight, creativity, humor, support, love, and faith have made all this possible. Thank you for being my teammate. I love you. Lastly and most importantly, I thank the Lord Jesus for making me more than who I am. You took the crumbs I had to offer and made something beautiful. May you receive all the glory and use this work to bring honor to your great Name.

Glossary of Terms

5 Whys: A method of root-cause analysis that entails the progressive asking of "Why?" at least five times or until the root cause is established.

6S: The principle of waste elimination through workplace organization. The five words are: *sort, straighten, scrub, systematize,* and *standardize. Safety* is often included as a sixth S.

Andon Cord: It is the concept that someone in the production process can stop movement to signal help or fix an issue.

Assets Waste: More inventory, physical resources, or information than needed or their misuse.

Capacity Waste: Failure to realize full potential and experience its benefits; capacity can be measured at both the individual and organizational levels.

Cohort: In the "check" step of PDCA, data is collected on different groups of customers. Each group is a cohort. In education, this can mean students separated into cohorts by ability, gender, etc.

Current State: An understanding that depicts things as they currently exist.

Customer: The person or entity who is the recipient of what you produce, either within your organization or outside your organization. The primary customer in education is the student.

Defects Waste: Work that contains errors, lacks something necessary, requires rework, or must be redone.

Error Proofing: A device or standard to prevent the production or occurrence of defects.

Flow: The ideal state where products move through a manufacturing process or people move through a service process one at a time, without stopping or waiting. In education this is the smooth, uninterrupted movement of students, supplies, and information.

Gemba: The place where value is added, where the action occurs. In education, this is the classroom or screen where a student is learning.

Ideal (Future) State: An improved view of the current state composed of only value-added activities.

Jidoka: This is quality at the source. Find defects and stop until the problem is fixed. This supports quality at the source and the prevention of defects from progressing. Additionally, the person in charge of the step is responsible to resolve the issue or stop the flow to get outside assistance. In education, both the instructor and student are responsible for quality learning.

Just inTime (JIT): Providing what is needed, when it is needed, in the quantity needed, and at the quality level needed.

Kaizen: Incremental continuous improvement that increases the effectiveness of an activity to produce more value with less waste.

Kanban: A signal that triggers replenishment or withdrawal in a pull system. The signal regulates the production flow. In education, this is a signal that a student has reached competency or achieved mastery of a topic or skill.

Knowledge Waste: Re-creating already existing knowledge.

Lean: An improvement methodology based on a customer-centric definition of value, and providing that value in the most effective way possible through a combination of the elimination of waste and a motivated and engaged workforce.

Learning Management System (LMS): Software application for the administration of educational courses.

Load Leveling: Doing approximately the same amount of work and exerting the same amount energy consistently over time and a throughout a process.

Minimum Viable Product: The smallest resource, product, or process possible to implement an improvement using the PDCA (Ries, 2011).

Movement Waste: Unnecessary physical movement, searching, or transportation of items or people which do not add value.

Overproduction Waste: Generating more of something or information than is needed right now, duplications, redundancies, unwarranted changes for the sake of change.

Plan Do Check Act (PDCA): An iterative improvement scheme at the core of the *kaizen* process. This four-step process includes (1) defining the objective, issues, and potential solution; (2) carrying out the plan in a trial mode; (3) verifying and studying trial results; and (4) fully implementing and standardizing the solution. This is the scientific process in a nutshell.

Prep: (1) An individual, different course an educator teaches; or (2) A period of time allotted during the teaching day for an educator to complete teaching tasks without students present.

Process and Handling Waste: Extra or unnecessary steps, reviews, approvals, or requirements, confusion.

Product: Good/service received by the customer. In education, the product is student learning.

Professional Learning Community (PLC): A group of teachers that work collaboratively for a shared content, student demographic, or grade level.

Pull: An entire process moving toward the customer at the rate the customer consumes a product. In education, this is a student learning to mastery at their own pace.

Respect for People: The engagement of and investment in people, including training, empowerment, safety, job security, contribution and respect of ideas, and morale. It is foundational to Lean and essential for the creation of a culture where *kaizen* (continuous improvement) thrives. Everyone is an expert in their position.

STEM: An acronym for fields of education: Science, Technology, Engineering, and Mathematics.

Split-test: An improvement is only offered to a select group to compare results with the group that did not receive the improvement.

Standardized Work: The definition of a process step characterized by a set work sequence. Deviations to standardized work constitute an abnormality, which is then an opportunity for improvement. Examples in education are procedures and classroom management.

Talent Waste: Not fully utilizing or developing the skills, training, and passion of staff and students. Limiting authority and responsibility for basic tasks.

Time Waste: Idle time created when actions, information, people, or equipment are not ready; excess or unwise use of time.

Value: The worth placed upon goods or services, as defined by the customer.

Value-added: Defined by the customer and must meet all the following criteria:

- The customer must be willing to "pay" for it. Payment is generally thought of in monetary terms, but could also include time or other resources. In education, this is a content or skill the student is to learn as prescribed by an educational authority.
- The product or service must be done correctly the first time.
- The product or service must be transformed.

Voice of the Customer (VOC): The collective needs, wants, and desires of the recipient of a process output, a product, or a service, whether expressed or not. The VOC is usually expressed as specification, requirements, or expectations. In education, a crucial part of the VOC is student feedback from the learning process.

Waste: Any activity that uses resources but creates no value for the customer. There are nine wastes in education: Assets, Capacity, Defects, Knowledge, Motion, Over Production, Process Handling, Talent, and Time (Lean Education Enterprises, Inc., 2007).

About the Author

Julie Laub is currently the Science Department Head and Advanced Placement/Concurrent Enrollment chemistry teacher at Davis High School and an adjunct professor at Weber State University for CHEM 1110. She earned her Bachelor of Science in Chemistry from the University of Utah and Master of Arts in Teaching Science from Western Governors University. She worked as an Organic Chemist in the semi-volatile GC/MS department for DataChem Laboratories upon college graduation.

Once beginning a family, she laid down her career to be a stay-at-home mom for her five beautiful daughters. In 2011, Julie entered the education world teaching chemistry at Clearfield High School. In 2012, she moved to Davis High School and has been voted teacher of the year many times and received district recognition as an outstanding educator. She simultaneously taught six years at the University of Utah in the CHEM 1070/1080 Labs and, in 2017, earned her Green Belt in Lean Six Sigma.

Julie hosts Lean Think workshops for state, district, and school personnel. She and her husband, Gregg, reside in Utah where faith, family, and teaching are the joys of her life. All she does revolves around those loves!

For more resources and workshop information visit LeanThink.org.

References

Best, M. a. (2006, April). Walter A Shewhart, 1924, and the Hawthorne factory. *Quality and Safety in Health Care*, pp. 142-143. Retrieved from Quality and Safety in Health Care: https://www.ncbi.nlm.nih.gov/pmc/articles/PMC2464836/

Casselman, B. a. (2017). Improving General Chemistry Course Performance through Online Homework-Based Metacognitive Training. *Journal of Chemical Education*, 1811-1821.

Clark, R. (2004). *The Essential 55*. Westport: Hyperion.

Dictionary, Y. (n.d.). *Your Dictionary Quotes*. Retrieved from Your Dictionary: https://quotes.yourdictionary.com/articles/who-said-a-penny-saved-is-a-penny-earned.html

Dweck, C. S. (2017). *Mindset*. Edinburgh: Robinson.

History of Space Pens. (2021). Retrieved from History of Pencils: http://www.historyofpencils.com/writing-instruments-history/history-of-space-pens/#:~:text=Space%20pen%20is%20a%20ballpoint,angle%20(even%20upside%20down).&text=He%20just%20wanted%20to%20make,which%20he%20patented%20in%201966.

Kondo, M. (2014). *The Life-Changing Magic of Tidying Up*. Berkeley: Ten Speed Press.

Lean Education Enterprises, Inc. (2007). The 9 Wastes in Education. *The 9 Wastes in Education*. St. Paul, MN, United States of America: Lean Education Enterprises, Inc.

Minahan, J. A. (2012). *Behavior Code: A Practical Guide to Understanding the Most Challenging Students*. Cambridge: Harvard Education Press.

Peterson, J. (2020, January 14). Choose Your Sacrifice. (A. Skool, Interviewer)

Ries, E. (2011). *The Lean Start Up*. New York: Crown Publishing.

Sayer, N. J. (2012). *Lean For Dummies*. Hoboken: John Wiley and Sons, Inc.

Schuett, D. (2016, January 28). *Skate to Where the Puck is Going - Position for the Future to Achieve a Competitive Edge*. Retrieved from Digital Reality Blog: https://www.digitalrealty.com/blog/skate-to-where-the-puck-is-going-position-for-the-future-to-achieve-a-competitive-edge

Smith, K. N. (2019, February 28). *Searching for the Ships Cortez Burned Before Destroying the Aztecs*. Retrieved from ARS Technica: https://arstechnica.com/science/2019/02/archaeologists-search-yucatan-coast-for-hernan-cortes-lost-ships/

Supermelon. (2021, January 5). *Taiicho Ohno Hero of the Toyota Production System*. Retrieved from Supermelon: https://supermelon.com/blog/post/taiichi-ohno-hero-of-the-toyota-production-system/

Womack, J. P. (1991). *The Machine that Changed the World*. New York: Free Press.

Wong, R. T. (1997). *The First Days of School: How to Be an Effective Teacher*. Mountain View: Harry K Wong Publishing.

Woods, R. (n.d.). *Manufacturing Survey Finds Widespread Use of Six Sigma, 5S, Kaizen*. Retrieved from ISixSigma: https://www.isixsigma.com/press-releases/manufacturing-survey-finds-widespread-use-lean-six-sigma-5s-kaizen/

Ziskovsky, B. a. (2010). *Optimizing Student Learning*. Milkaukee: ASQ Quality Press.